Earth's Growing Population

Education Resource Center
University of Delaware
Newark, DE 19716-2940

ENVIRONMENT AT RISK

Earth's Growing Population

CHRIS REITER

Marshall Cavendish
Benchmark
New York

Other Marshall Cavendish Offices:
Marshall Cavendish International (Asia) Private Limited, 1 New Industrial Road, Singapore 536196 •
Marshall Cavendish International (Thailand) Co Ltd. 253 Asoke, 12th Flr, Sukhumvit 21 Road, Klongtoey
Nua, Wattana, Bangkok 10110, Thailand • Marshall Cavendish (Malaysia) Sdn Bhd, Times Subang, Lot 46,
Subang Hi-Tech Industrial Park, Batu Tiga, 40000 Shah Alam, Selangor Darul Ehsan, Malaysia

Marshall Cavendish is a trademark of Times Publishing Limited
All websites were available and accurate when this book was sent to press.

Library of Congress Cataloging-in-Publication Data
Reiter, Chris.
Earth's growing population / Chris Reiter.
p. cm. — (Environment at risk)
Includes bibliographical references and index.
Summary: "Provides comprehensive information on population growth and its effects on the
environment"—Provided by publisher.
ISBN 978-1-60870-481-1 (print) — ISBN 978-1-60870-678-5 (ebook)
1. Population—Environmental aspects. 2. Population—Economic aspects. 3. Natural resources—
Management. 4. Environmental economics. I. Title.
HC79.E5R4483 2012
304.6'2—dc22
2010046784

Editor: Christine Florie
Publisher: Michelle Bisson
Art Director: Anahid Hamparian
Series Designer: Sonia Chaghatzbanian

Expert Reader: Lori M. Hunter, Ph.D., Associate Professor of Sociology and Environmental Studies, Institute
of Behavioral Science, Programs on Population, Environment and Society, Editor-in-Chief *Population and
Environment*, University of Colorado at Boulder

Photo research by Marybeth Kavanagh

Cover photo by *Clive Sawyer PCL/SuperStock*
The photographs in this book are used by permission and through the courtesy of: *SuperStock*: Clive
Sawyer PCL, 1; Stock Connection, 9; Eye Ubiquitous, 46, 51, 55; All Canada Photos, 48; Prisma, 49, 83;
Robert Harding Picture Library, 62; *Alamy*: The Guardian, 2-3, 4; Mark Shenley, 6; Charlotte Thege,
17; INTERFOTO, 27; North Wind Picture Archives, 36; Peter Arnold, Inc., 76; Rich Iwasaki, 89; *Getty
Images*: Annie Griffiths Belt/National Geographic, 13; Buyenlarge, 31; Three Lions, 34; Rob Shone/Dorling
Kindersley, 43; Jay Directo/AFP, 67; U.S. Coast Guard, 82; *Newscom*: Bro-Jorgensen/MCT, 15; Musser/MCT,
37; *The Image Works*: Lightroom Photos/NASA/Topham, 22; Bob Daemmrich, 45; David R. Frazier, 64;
Eastcott/Momatiuk, 65; Richard B. Levine/GreenStockMedia, 88; *North Wind Picture Archives*: 28; *Everett
Collection*, Inc.: 40; *AP Photo*: Sayyid Azim, 74; *Cutcaster*: Yuri Arcurs, back cover, 1, 2, 10, 11, 18, 19, 30, 31,
37, 52, 56, 57, 70, 71, 75, 84, 85, 92, 93

Printed in Malaysia (T)
1 3 5 6 4 2

Contents

One

A Crowded House

Just after dawn on a sultry morning in early May, a young man leaves his family's failing farm in the Nigerian countryside and sets out across acres of dusty sorghum fields for Lagos, West Africa's largest city and one of the fastest-growing cities in the world.

For impoverished Nigerians, Lagos is a beacon of opportunity. There are glittering skyscrapers and international banks, busy marketplaces, and a world-renowned music scene. But, for most, Lagos will offer little relief. Swelling day by day with new migrants and newborn children, the city is bursting at the seams. Since 1950, the population of Lagos has grown from a modest 300,000 to nearly 15 million, and the city government, desperately overwhelmed, cannot meet the basic needs of its people.

Clean water is scarce in Lagos. Sewage regularly flows into rivers and bays. Children sift through mountainous garbage

As many of the world's rural regions struggle with poverty, millions of people are migrating to cities, such as Lagos, Nigeria (left), where population growth is surging.

heaps for food, clothing, and cast-off computer parts, hustling to make ends meet. There are even floating slums, worn-out docks and barges with makeshift shelters made of plastic tarps, salvaged plywood, and scraps of tin. Schools and hospitals are just a dream. For the people of Lagos, and for more than one billion people worldwide living on less than a dollar a day, this is life in a crowded world.

Life in rural Nigeria is difficult, too. In a mere fifty years, the country's population, the largest in Africa, has grown from 45 million to 160 million. But, as in the city, the natural systems that support life across Nigeria cannot sustain such rapid growth. Human needs collide with the limits of the land. Crops of wheat, millet, sorghum, and yams, which once provided sufficient food, now provide too little nourishment for too many. Desperate to grow more food, farmers overuse their fields, exhausting the nutrients in the soil. An extended drought caused by climate change makes matters worse. There are dust bowls and withering crops, shortages of food and water, and in 2010, a cholera epidemic.

Nigeria is not alone. Many countries are experiencing rapid population growth as millions of people migrate from rural areas to increasingly crowded cities, like Lagos. In fact, these are global trends with so much momentum that it is difficult to conceive the scope and speed of population change. In an article for *Development Express*, writer Mario Polese reports that in 1900 most of the world's population, roughly 1.5 billion people, lived in rural areas; only 150 million people lived in cities, and only a few were cities larger than one million people. By 2000 there were 2.9 billion urban dwellers, and in 2008 demographers for the United Nations Population Fund determined that half the world's population lived in cities. Another branch of the United Nations projects that by 2015 there will be twenty-seven cities worldwide with populations exceeding 10 million Tokyo alone has a population of 35 million, greater than the entire population of Canada.

These megacities, the capitals of hypergrowth, are found in developed and developing nations. Joining Tokyo are cities such as Los Angeles, Cairo, Mexico City, Istanbul, and Mumbai, all growing at a dizzying rate. Add to the rise of the megacities the ongoing growth of rural populations in many poor countries, and a global phenomenon of vast proportions arises: a momentous surge in world population.

It took roughly 12,000 years, from the Neolithic Age to 1800, for the human population to rise from 4 million to one billion people. In less than two hundred years, in 1960, there were 3 billion people on Earth. By October 1999 world population had doubled to 6 billion. By 2012, according to the U.S. Census Bureau, our numbers will likely surpass 7 billion.

The population of Tokyo swells with urban dwellers, making this Japanese city one of the most populous in the world.

Megacity Miracles

Life in megacities like Lagos is not easy. The poverty, the overcrowding, the daily struggle for food and water can be grueling. But urbanization is by no means all bad. Many people, fleeing extreme poverty, find jobs, go to school for the first time, and begin to build better lives. And megacities' daunting problems can also inspire creativity and positive change. When Jaime Lerner was mayor of Curitiba, Brazil, he led the creation of innovative, low-tech social programs, including gardens tended by street kids, payments in food to homeless people who collect litter, and converted buses that serve as mobile health clinics in the slums. Mayor Lerner also oversaw the building of dozens of community libraries, so many that no child in the city has to walk more than 12 minutes to reach one.

He offered architectural assistance to poor immigrants building their own homes. Lerner also had built an efficient, inexpensive mass transit system and created acres of new parks and tree-lined boulevards, giving it the most green space of any city in Brazil.

As detailed in the environmental design sourcebook *WorldChanging*, making megacities work will take mega-creativity. The writers believe that two-thirds of the urban areas that will cover the planet in 2030 do not yet exist, and they will not look like anything we have ever seen. They are unfolding in places where people have mobile phones but still use mule-driven carts to travel and move goods; places that sell computer chips in outdoor farmers' markets and places where young people worship in five-hundred-year-old temples but follow video game championships on TV. It's a new world, an urban future being created by a generation just now coming into its own.

What Numbers Tell Us

All these numbers, these billions upon billions, can be overwhelming. The cold, hard facts pile up. The statistics are staggering. How does one grasp the phenomenon of 7 billion human souls sharing the planet? How can a city of 35 million meet the everyday needs of its citizens? And what, after all, does the exploding population of São Paulo have to do with life in Boston or Chicago or Seattle? What can numbers really tell us about our lives, the lives of others, and the state of our world? Actually, quite a lot.

Demographers, those who study population change and population growth, are sometimes thought of as mere bean counters. But the statistics demographers compile are a way of measuring and understanding changes in the world that affect the life of every living thing on Earth, from the young man on his way to Lagos to the individuals in any given community to the plants and animals in the rain forests in Indonesia and the Amazon.

In fact, the study of population change, close to home and around the world, educates us about the most pressing environmental and social challenges of our time. Alleviating poverty, improving public health, addressing climate change, supporting women's rights, protecting biodiversity and the health of the air, water, and soil—all are linked to population growth, and all affect our common future.

Most of those who study sustainability—our ability to meet today's human needs while protecting the wealth and health of the Earth for future generations—believe that population growth adds an acute sense of urgency to these challenges. In a crowded world, there is enormous pressure on the Earth's capacity to provide a healthy, satisfying life for everyone. The consumption of food, water, and energy, and the ever-growing demand for the materials used to build homes and cars, highways and cities, are threatening to take more from the Earth than the Earth has to give.

Consider Los Angeles, one of North America's most populous cities. Home to 28 million people, Los Angeles occupies an arid coastal desert that can sustainably supply fresh water

The effects of providing the American West with water can be seen on the Colorado River. Dried by irrigation needs, it no longer flows through its delta.

for roughly one million people. To quench the city's thirst, dozens of dams, countless reservoirs, and some 700 miles of canals, tunnels, and pipelines deliver billions of gallons of water to Los Angeles from distant rivers and aquifers. Much of it comes from the Colorado River, which supplies so much water to the cities of the American West that it no longer flows into the Gulf of Mexico; it simply slows to a trickle in the desert and dries out. The Colorado River's wetlands, once rich in biodiversity, have virtually disappeared. Climate change and drought take a further toll, shrinking already overtaxed reservoirs. During the spring of 2010, drinking water was in such short supply in Los Angeles that the LA City Council

considered a strict water-rationing plan, and California gover- nor Arnold Schwarzenegger ordered a 20 percent cut in water usage statewide.

Underground aquifers, a source of water used to irrigate desert farmlands, are also running dry. In California's arid Central Valley, a land that would not naturally support the growth of strawberries and lettuce, irrigation and fertilizers are widely used to make the soil suitable for crops. But fertilizer, while adding nutrients to the soil, also is leached into streams, rivers, and aquifers, poisoning the very source of the drinking water that is in such short supply.

With all these heavy demands, Los Angeles's ever-growing population has profoundly disrupted the water cycle of an entire region. In ecologists' terms, this is a case of a city's ecological footprint overwhelming the carrying capacity of the natural systems upon which it depends. The ecological footprint is the total environmental impact of human activity in a particular place. A "footprint" can measure human impact on many scales, from a single household to an entire nation. *Carrying capacity* refers to the capacity of an ecosystem to sustainably support life over time. When a population's ecological footprint exceeds an ecosystem's carrying capacity, it is said that the population has overreached.

The Logic of Sustainability: Easing Human Pressure on the Environment
Overreaching is not uncommon. According to the UN Ecosystem Assessment, a four-year United Nations study conducted by 1,360 of the world's leading scientists, "human activity is putting such strain on the natural functions of Earth that the ability of the planet's ecosystems to sustain future generations can no longer be taken for granted." How, then, do we meet the needs of every human being while preserving the vitality of the Earth? With 6 billion people and counting, 83 million births a year, how do we create a just, richly diverse, sustainable world?

There are no easy answers. But many environmental thinkers agree that there is a fundamental "logic of sustainability,"

Global ecosystem suffering

Demands on Earth's natural resources are almost one-third more than it can sustain, World Wildlife Fund report says.

National ecological footprint

Amount of the Earth's land and sea needed to provide the resources used, in hectares per person:

| <2 | 2-4 | 4-6 | >6 | Insufficient data |

National biocapacities* (As percentage of world total, 2005)

U.S.	11.2%
Brazil	10.1%
Russia	8.7%
China	8.5%
Canada	4.8%
India	3.4%
Argentina	2.4%
Australia	2.3%
Indonesia	2.3%
D. R. Congo	1.8%

Top 10 nations 55.5%

Other nations 44.5%

*Biocapacity is an area's ability to generate an ongoing supply of renewable resources; unsustainability occurs if the area's ecological footprint exceeds its biocapacity

Source: WWF Living Planet Report 2008; GreenFacts
Graphic: Junie Bro-Jorgensen   © 2008 MCT

Results of a 2008 study by the World Wildlife Fund's "The Living Planet Report," shows that demands on natural resources overreach what Earth can sustain by almost one-third.

15

a clear way of thinking about the collision between population growth and the well-being of the planet. The path is simple: increasing numbers have increasing needs. Increasing needs drive overconsumption. Overconsumption disrupts the ecological processes on which humanity and countless other species depend. Therefore, if we balance population growth and dramatically reduce consumption, we can meet human needs and create a more sustainable relationship with the Earth.

A leading scholar of population change, Robert Engelman, says, "Population growth constantly pushes the consequences of any level of individual consumption to a higher plateau, and reductions in individual consumption can always be overwhelmed by increases in population." He states "the simple reality" is that acting on both population growth and overconsumption, "consistently and simultaneously, is the key to long-term environmental sustainability. . . . The benefits of level or falling numbers are too powerful to ignore."

Most environmental scholars believe that Engelman's ideas are sound. Most also agree that they will be very difficult to put into practice. In the real world, where political and personal choices are made, the logic of sustainability is often turned on its head. In fact, differences in circumstance can make one person's logic seem positively illogical to another. There are cultural differences, such as those that affect a woman's freedom to choose whether to have children. There are differences between the opportunities and freedoms of the wealthy and those of the impoverished. There are clashing ideologies both between and within nations. When populations migrate they change both the places they leave and those that become their new homes. These differences, and many others, make the choices that affect population growth and sustainability difficult to influence and impossible to predict.

The Big Three
The nations with the largest populations on Earth, the "big three," are India, the United States, and China. Their fertility patterns provide interesting contrasts.

Consider a story from India. A young woman nearly dies delivering her eighth baby. Three of her children have died, and another pregnancy may jeopardize her life. Nevertheless, her husband and [her] mother-in-law want her to try for another son—a highly prized asset in traditional Indian culture."

But India's traditional culture does not dominate the entire country. Many women are far more empowered than those valued solely for childbearing. Those who are educated and employed can enjoy the benefits of a growing economy. Many women hold positions of power in government and industry. If they choose to have children, they plan their families with their partners and tend to have fewer children than their parents and grandparents. In portions of India, and across the world, women are gaining the freedom to shape their lives. Their childbearing is fully intentional.

Still, tradition dies hard. In spite of India's new prosperity, there is still intense pressure on young married couples to

In rural areas of impoverished countries, where many women die in childbirth, large families are highly valued; with mortality rates high, having several children ensures that there will be enough help with farmwork and caring for the elderly.

Great Migrations

People have always been on the move. The number moving to cities now is unprecedented, but migration has always been a big part of population change. In fact, the entire world was settled by successive migrations from Africa.

The first great migration within the United States occurred between 1915 and 1930, when nearly 2 million African Americans left the South. After 1930 the migration slowed, but by 1970, 6 million had left their homes, most moving to northern cities. They were fleeing the so-called Jim Crow laws enacted after 1880, which legalized segregation in the South. Georgia was the first state to pass a Jim Crow law, ordering separate seating for whites and blacks in streetcars. In 1896 the Supreme Court ruled, in *Plessy v. Ferguson*, that segregation was constitutional. A flood of segregation laws followed the ruling. Segregation came to trains, restaurants, movie theaters, churches, schools, hospitals, almost every public space. The inequality and hardships of segregation were unbearable, and African Americans who could leave the South did. In search of good jobs, freedom, and dignity, they went to New York City, Chicago, Philadelphia, Detroit, and other urban areas in the North and West.

This mass migration changed America. Chicago became the home of the blues. Harlem became a lively, vibrant center of jazz, poetry, theater, and art. Professional sports teams in the North were the first to hire black athletes. Ultimately, African Americans influenced every sphere of American life. The traditional cultures of black and white became inseparably entwined.

Before and after African Americans moved north, millions of people from all over the world moved to the United States, and migrations to America have never stopped. However, not everyone has been pleased. Throughout the nineteenth and twentieth centuries laws were passed to control immigration, but they slowed rather than halted migrations from the rest of the world. At the same time, many people took pride in the United States being a "melting pot" of civilizations and saw diversity as a source of national strength. Always, there have been strenuous debates about immigration. Whatever side one argues, there is a rich history to consult.

prove their fertility. And poverty exerts its own pressure. Poor, uneducated women, often struggling with ill health, tend to have more children than prosperous women. The poor want to be sure that at least one or two children reach adulthood to help with farming or other labor-intensive work. Also, family planning is often not accessible, is likely to be financially out of reach, and may be forbidden by custom. As a result, the average Indian woman still bears three to four children; the worldwide average is 2.6 children. In 2010 India's population surpassed 1.5 billion. Within decades, India will be the most populous nation on Earth.

Born in the USA
A child is born in New York City. She is her parents' first child and will perhaps be their only one. Within an hour of her birth, 228 more children will be born in the United States; within a day, nearly 5,500. If this birthrate is set against the country's death rate, the resulting ratio is considered to represent relatively slow population growth, which is typical in wealthy nations. As in the parts of India where education, employment, and health care are readily available, many American women favor fully intentional childbirth, and most decide to have one or two children.

Even so, the United States has population issues. From 1900 to 2010 the U.S. population grew from 76 million to 310 million. Though the U.S. birthrate is not explosive, the population will continue to grow. That's not shocking, comparatively speaking, but the gargantuan rate of consumption in the United States aggravates the problems of population growth, not just in the United States but around the world.

In fact, the average American consumes twenty-five times more resources than the average person from a developing nation. Put another way, the United States, with 5 percent of the world's population, consumes more than 20 percent of the world's natural capital, the materials and services provided by the earth. As Robert Engelman writes, "in this unequal world, the behavior of a dozen people in one place sometimes has more environmental impact than does that of a few hundred somewhere else."

Taste the Fun

China, the third nation in the "big three," has its own particular dilemmas with population and consumption. Because of its immense size, they are world-changing dilemmas; China may either blow down the house or rebuild it.

With a population of 1.5 billion, China has a supersized ecological footprint, far larger than its carrying capacity. It reaches out to nations all over the world, from South America to Africa, for the resources it needs to fuel its vast, fast-growing economy. At the same time, China has made a significant commitment to sustainability, working hard to cut its carbon emissions, the heat-trapping gases that cause climate change, and to increase its energy efficiency. In 2010 the Chinese government showed just how serious it is about sustainability: it shut down two thousand factories that were failing to meet stringent energy-efficiency goals.

But China is also recovering from a century of dire poverty, and as the fortunes of its large and growing population rise, so does the nation's impact on the environment. Consider the growth of China's car culture. In late August 2010, on a highway between Mongolia and Beijing, a tangle of cars and trucks squeezing into the capital city came to a virtual standstill, backing up for 60 miles and stalling traffic for more than ten days. Traffic was so jammed that some cars and trucks moved little more than a mile a day; on other days, not at all. Drivers got out of their cars and slept on the side of the road. Others left their vehicles to play cards, take long walks, talk on their cell phones, and trade their belongings for food and water.

No one was terribly surprised. Beijing is the traffic-jam capital of the world. And China is car crazy. Hundreds of thousands of new drivers hit the road every year. In Beijing alone, more than a thousand new cars roll onto the streets every day. The air is thick with exhaust and pollution, but China's new middle class wants to enjoy its prosperity and "taste the fun" of owning a car. Zhu Chao, a young website designer, loves driving around with his friends. As he told the *Washington Post*, "I really like what the car brings to my life—convenience,

21

As China has grown, its demand for electricity, generated mostly by coal-power fired plants, has greatly increased. This satellite image shows a thick layer of haze over eastern China.

freedom, flexibility, a quick rhythm. I can't imagine life without it."

China's economic growth, the most explosive economic boom in the history of the world, has lifted millions out of poverty. But Beijing's exhaust sickens its people and drifts thousands of miles across the Pacific, all the way to the American

Midwest. China has designed and built thousands of afford-able electric cars, the world's largest fleet; but it also leads the world in carbon emissions. So it is that against the grain of our hopes, a nation rising out of poverty must also meet the sur-vival needs of a fast-growing population, aggravating the world's most pressing environmental problems.

Sharing the Wealth

So goes the vexing relationship between population and sustainability. The conventional wisdom, and all the research, says that economic development brings more opportun-ities for women, lower birthrates, population balance, and a greater chance for a sustainable relationship with the Earth. But China's growth and its giant ecological footprint seem to contradict the evidence. Are we already too many? Do over-consumption, as in the United States, and sheer numbers, as in China, upend the possibility or a prosperous, sustainable world?

Not surprisingly, everyone wants to share the wealth. Young people in Karachi, Jakarta, and Lagos want to live like young Americans. Not only do they want to be free of hunger and illness, but they also want to "taste the fun" and experi-ence the "freedom, flexibility, and quick rhythm" enjoyed by Mr. Zhu Chao, the young car enthusiast in China. They want, as we all do, to enjoy health, opportunity, and good fortune.

Pessimists say that's unlikely, even impossible. They say that the poor will always be with us, and if the world's devel-oping nations were to follow in the footsteps of the United States, we would need five times the resources currently used by the entire world. A pessimist might say, and a very level-headed environmental scientist might agree, that population growth cannot be balanced soon enough to halt an earthshak-ing collision between human numbers and human needs. Eco-logical collapse is inevitable.

An often-quoted United Nations statement published in 2002, the Johannesburg Memo, puts it succinctly: "There is no escape from the conclusion that the world's growing popula-tion can not attain a Western standard of living by following conventional paths to development. The resources required are

too vast, too expensive, and too damaging to local and global ecosystems."

Exactly, says the optimist. That's why we need to create a new model of development. We don't have to follow in the oversized footsteps of the United States and China. We can balance human needs with what the Earth has to give. We can make the world work for everyone.

If this scenario sounds overly optimistic, it is certainly not an idle dream. Literally millions of people, in every arena of life—business, politics, science, architecture, agriculture, medicine, education, philanthropy, and more—have given their hearts and minds and energy to creating such a world. Many, for good reason, are doing so by studying population growth. Clearly, population growth underlies many of the most pressing environmental and social challenges of our time. It is entwined in each of our lives and affects our common future.

Two

The Rise and Fall of Populations

Agriculture and technology have always fueled the rise and fall of populations. For millennia, the abundance or shortage of food has given and taken good health, built and broken civilizations, and inspired new technologies. These cycles of plenty and hunger, of bountiful fields and withering crops, tell a story that links a sparsely populated world of simple farmers to today's industrialized world of nearly 7 billion. It's a story about the many ways in which we have grown and shared food, and how, for good or ill, we developed technologies that have changed the Earth.

Irrigation, for example, allowed farmers to cultivate larger fields and grow more food, which in turn fed larger populations. Plentiful food also gave people time to think and invent, sustaining the creative thought that led to writing, science, engineering, and ever more complex technologies. Populous civilizations were possible because agriculture and technology walked hand in hand, an advance in one leading to an advance in the other. Rome wasn't built on an empty stomach.

Still, at the present moment, when more than a billion people suffer from extreme hunger, and upward of 3 billion are malnourished, the story of our relationship to food and technology is more meaningful than ever.

Peopling the Earth

Ten thousand years ago there were only ten thousand people on Earth. They lived in small, widely scattered groups, sometimes no larger than extended families. The quest for food defined their lives. With determined, single-minded effort, they hunted wild game and gathered fruits, grains, seeds, and greens. The challenge of food gathering cultivated sharp minds and keen attention. Watching seeds sprout and grow, the hunter-gatherers learned the life cycles of plants and began to return each year to the places where they could collect their favorite foods.

In subtle ways they worked the land. They dug tubers and roots, cleared small patches of prairie for sun-loving plants, and began to save seeds and sow them in another season or place. In time, seed gatherers all over the world—in the Middle East, India, China, Africa, and the Americas—would plant and cultivate fields of wheat, barley, lentils, peas, maize, and rice. These would become the first crops intentionally sown, cultivated, and harvested on a large scale.

Agriculture changed the world. Early farming in fertile soils produced a vast surplus of grains, an abundance of food unknown to hunter-gathers. Places with especially good harvests drew people together in farming villages. Eventually, domesticated animals added meat, milk, and cheese to the sturdy diet of cereal grains. Working cooperatively, farming peoples produced ever more food, which fed ever larger settlements. By 3000 BCE, some had become powerful engines of food production, growing into densely populated, highly organized cities. In Egypt around 2000 BCE, a single urban warehouse held enough grain to feed 20,000 people for a full year.

Technology drove the evolution of agriculture, just as it drives change today. People in Mesopotamia, the lands between the Tigris and Euphrates rivers in the Middle East, harnessed the power of water. They drained swamps and irrigated their crops, cut flood channels and canals, built dams and reservoirs, and constructed machines for carrying water from rivers to upstream fields. They channeled water to moisten dry soil,

An ancient Egyptian mural depicts the harvesting of grain. Agriculture was a foundation of population growth at that time.

giving life to apples, plums, olives, figs, lettuce, melons, and dates, as well as cereal grains. This stable, diverse diet nourished a thriving civilization.

In each place where technology provided more food, populations grew. In ancient Sumer, in present-day Iraq, irrigated land supported a network of twelve city-states. Uruk, the first true metropolis, was home to no less than 40,000 people. Nineveh, a prosperous city on the Tigris River, had a population of 120,000. Babylon, a settlement on the Euphrates River, was an especially impressive city. There, people used writing, counting, and mathematics to keep track of harvests, livestock, and surplus grain. Babylonians developed weights and measures and multiplication tables. They developed geometry to calculate the area of fields and the structure of dams. They created what might have been the very first census, to count their growing population. From these advances in agriculture

Technology and sophisticated agriculture supported the growth of large, populous cities in ancient Mesopotamia.

and technology came mathematics, science, and engineering, the foundations of knowledge that have sustained growing populations for centuries.

Collapse

Yet the cities of Mesopotamia collapsed. The very technologies that allowed them to prosper brought on their decline. As well-fed populations grew, so did the cities' need for water and food. Because more and more water was being drawn from the rivers to irrigate larger fields, the act of farming dried up the deltas. Without regular flows of floodwater, the irrigation canals filled with eroding soil. The rich irrigated farmlands returned to desert, and the food supply nearly vanished.

In spite of all their achievements, the Mesopotamian civilizations had overreached. The needs of their growing populations had overwhelmed the Earth's ability to provide sustenance. In ecologists' terms, those ancient peoples had exceeded the carrying capacity of their environment. When a population balances its needs with the services nature provides—plentiful water, clean air, fertile soil—it is living within the means of its environment. Both the population and the Earth's natural systems are healthy and sustainable. If a population overshoots its carrying capacity, that's when trouble begins.

The concept of carrying capacity was unknown to the people of Mesopotamia. They were simply using imagination and ingenuity to create more stable, comfortable lives. Motivated by a desire to prosper and thrive, they remade the landscape to meet their needs. Unfortunately, their mistakes have been repeated again and again.

Populations grow when people prosper. Sustained by new technologies, human populations have grown for millennia. During the late years of the hunter-gathers, world population was one million. By 4000 BCE, after the evolution of farming, it had grown to 7 million. In 3000 BCE, following the rise of the Middle Eastern cultures of Sumer and Babylon, the population of the planet had doubled to roughly 14 million.

Though agriculture failed in Mesopotamia, it thrived in China and India and the Americas, fueling new population growth. In 2000 BCE, world population approached 27 million. At the time of Moses, a thousand years later, it had increased to 50 million. In the first year of the Common Era, two thousand years ago, there were 250 million people on Earth. In China alone, which developed its own sophisticated farming techniques, a sparse, nomadic population grew to 60 million by the twelfth century CE. Today, after astonishing advances in agriculture and technology, the Earth is home to 6.9 billion people. All this from ten thousand hunter-gathers, living independently in roving bands.

Why Counting Counts

The first censuses, those in ancient Egypt and Babylonia, were taken mostly out of concern for property and wealth. They provided information about the number of people who were

The Sodbusters

Ancient Mesopotamia is another world, separated from us in almost every way. But the Great American Dust Bowl of the mid–1930s showed how, in some very important ways, little has changed in thousands of years: we are still trying to figure out how to grow food without laying waste to the natural world.

At its peak the Dust Bowl covered 100 million acres (40,470,000 hectares) of prairie in parts of Texas, Colorado, Kansas, Oklahoma, and New Mexico. This vast tract of land, which had been used for grazing for many years, began to come undone when farmers plowed the prairie sod to grow wheat for East Coast markets. It was an area prone to drought and high winds. Without the sod, the unprotected soil turned to dust, and when high winds blew in 1934, they blasted the soil of the High Plains around the world. Author Timothy Egan captures the moment vividly:

> Dust clouds boiled up, ten thousand feet or more into the sky, and rolled like moving mountains—a force of their own. When the dust fell it penetrated everything: hair, nose, throat, kitchen, bedroom. . . . The eeriest thing was the darkness. People tied themselves to ropes before going to a barn just a few hundred feet away. . . . A storm in May 1934 carried the

windblown shards of the Great Plains over much of the nation. In Chicago, 12 million tons of dust fell. New York, Washington—even ships at sea, three hundred miles off the Atlantic Coast—were blanketed in brown. . . . On April 14, 1935, a storm carried twice as much dirt as was dug out of the earth to create the Panama Canal.

The Great Plains soil was so ravaged that 3 million people left their farms and moved west, many to California. Yet the American Dust Bowl pales in comparison to present-day dust bowls in Africa and Asia. In the arid provinces of China, for example, advancing deserts could displace tens of millions of people.

available for labor and how many cattle and sheep were in an emperor's corrals. The Roman Empire counted its citizens to enable the calculation of its manpower for conquest and its annual revenue from taxes.

Today, counting populations is still a way of taking stock. The focus has changed, and the methods demographers use are far more sophisticated; but a census is still a way of figuring out where we stand. As we have seen, the tracking of rising populations in the past reveals the significance of technology in human history, which can tell us something about our future.

In our time, scientists and scholars who study population growth are most concerned with where we stand in relation to the Earth. They want not only to learn how population change is affecting ecosystems and biodiversity but also to determine its effects on poverty and hunger. They are concerned with measuring and understanding the ways in which our growing numbers have put both people and the planet at risk. They gather data and crunch numbers to help us imagine ways to create a safe, just, and prosperous future.

Numbers tell stories, and comparing numbers tells better stories. If we count the number of people in the United States, for example, we know how many people live there at a particular time. That's interesting, but it doesn't tell us very much. However, if we regularly count the population every ten years, we can measure change. Did the population rise or fall?

More questions bring more information. How many people in the population are women? How many are men? Are there more twelve-year-olds than people older than sixty-five? How is the population distributed from state to state? How many people earn more than $50,000 each year? How many less? How many are malnourished? How many go to school? How much water do we use? How much land is used for farming? The more questions we ask, the better our picture of a place in time. The data, in turn, can be compared to statistics from other places, sketching an even more informative picture of a region or a nation or the world.

How We Count

Populations are always in flux, but population change can be understood by using a few basic measurements. For example, fertility rate and mortality rate are two fundamental concepts used to measure the rise and fall of populations. The combination of high fertility rates with low mortality rates means that a population is growing. In other words, the number of newborns at a given time is greater than the number of people who died during that period.

The rate of growth, the number of people added to a population from year to year, indicates how fast the population is increasing. At the replacement level, populations neither rise nor fall numerically; the number of newborns at a given time is roughly equal to the number of people who died during that period. Thus, the fertility rate of a population at the replacement level is roughly 2.1—enough children to replace two parents, and account for a low level of child mortality. When this occurs, a population is stable, a condition known as zero population growth. When the fertility rate exceeds the replacement level while the mortality rate is stable—more children, fewer people dying—the rate of growth gains speed. At high speed, when the rate of birth exceeds the death rate over an extended period, populations are said to be experiencing exponential growth.

Exponential growth picks up speed from generation to generation. For example, when two parents contribute three children to a population (that is, more than the replacement rate of 2.1) and those three children grow up to have three children apiece of their own, each generation is 50 percent larger than the one that came before. At this rate, population growth takes off and begins to double, which adds up to astonishing numbers over time. From 1804 to 1960 world population grew from one billion to 3 billion. We are now nearing 7 billion. That's exponential growth.

Populations also bulge. The baby boom in the United States is a good example. During the baby boom, a period of roughly fifteen years following World War II, the population of the United States surged. It was a time of economic prosperity,

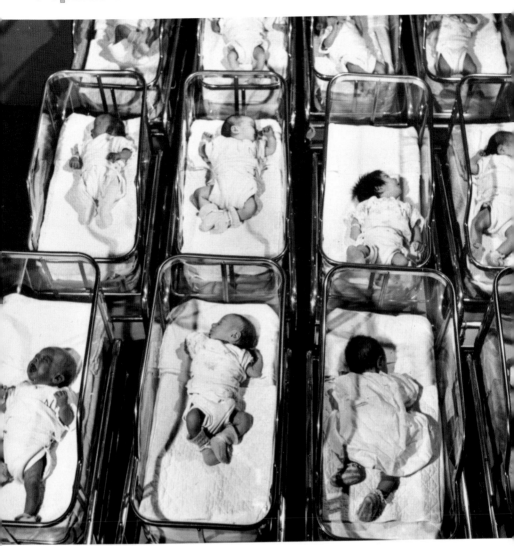

From 1946 through 1964, a time of U.S. economic wealth, the population in America grew in vast numbers.

when new technologies provided abundant food, energy, and comfort to many Americans. Prosperity offered a newfound sense of security and gave people the means to support more children. Advances in medicine, meanwhile, allowed elderly Americans to live much longer. As a result, the U.S. population boomed, growing by 76 million between 1946 and 1964.

A bulge like the baby boom creates population momentum. Even if the rate of growth slows, there are so many more people having children that the overall population continues to grow.

Clearly, numbers matter. And they matter most when growing numbers collide with the limits of the natural world. Centuries ago, Mesopotamia's collision with the natural world brought down civilizations. And a more catastrophic collision was yet to come.

A Population Explosion

Population growth spurred by early agriculture was amazing, but the next population explosion, beginning around 1750, was earth shattering. So earth shattering, in fact, that we continue to feel the reverberations today. Just as in early civilizations, advances in agriculture and technology paved the way. Only this time the massive change they spurred came about in decades rather than millennia. This rapid change, unprecedented in human history, was the Industrial Revolution. The world it created, for good and ill, is the world we live in today.

The Industrial Revolution took root in the farmlands of northern Europe, especially in England. There, farmers turned agriculture into a science. Rotating crops, using fertilizer, and experimenting with new kinds of grain, they produced an extraordinary surplus of food. It was a stable surplus because the new methods of farming preserved the health of the soil. The vast food supply spurred rapid population growth. Farming became so efficient that fewer laborers were required, and a growing number of people left the countryside in search of jobs. In booming cities like London, they joined a workforce that powered new industries and enterprises.

These industries, such as the manufacturing of wool and cotton cloth, were driven by a quick succession of new technologies. Machines for spinning and weaving yarn increased the pace of production. In 1790, for example, ten times as much cotton yarn was generated than had been just twenty years earlier. By 1840 factories that had produced a thousand pieces a week were turning out a thousand a day. With food

The Industrial Revolution was a time of great change. As agriculture and industrial technology developed, families grew as well, as can be seen in this illustration of an 1870 New York schoolroom.

plentiful and cheap, many people had the means to support more children. Population grew as quickly as industry.

Rapid change became a world-changing revolution when industrialists harnessed a new form of energy, fossil fuel. Economist Jeffrey Sachs aptly describes this dramatic moment:

> The steam engine marked the decisive turning point of modern history. By mobilizing a vast store of primary energy, fossil fuels, the steam engine unlocked the mass production of goods and services on a scale beyond the wildest dreams of the preindustrial era. Modern energy fueled every aspect of the economic takeoff. Food production soared as fossil fuel energy was used to produce chemical fertilizers; industrial production skyrocketed as vast inputs of fossil fuel energy created equally vast powerhouses of steel, transport equipment, chemicals and pharmaceuticals, textile and apparels, and every other modern

World Population

The rate of population growth in the last two hundred years is a novelty. For most of the last two thousand years, population growth was gradual, rising very slowly over time. Then it surged in 1800, along with economic growth, and has been surging ever since. The rate of growth peaked in the 1970s, but because population growth had so much momentum—more people around to have children—our numbers continue to rise today.

Global population to reach 7 billion by 2012

There are 6.7 billion people in the world today. According to Census Bureau projections, the world population will reach 7 billion in just 4 years, and nearly 10 billion by 2050.

© 2008 MCT
Source: Noah Musser,
The Kansas City Star
Graphic: AP, U.S. Census
Bureau, Infoplease.com

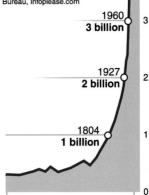

World population in billions

2050
9.5 billion

2012
7 billion

1960
3 billion

1927
2 billion

1804
1 billion

1000

2000

manufacturing sector. By the early 20th century . . .
modern information and communications technologies were powered by electricity, itself a break-
through of the fossil fuel age.

Global population soared hand in hand with advances in
agriculture, science, and technology. Birthrates rose, mortality rates dropped, and rates of growth accelerated, building
unprecedented momentum.

Demographic Transition

During the population explosion, economic growth differed
from country to country. The benefits of the Industrial Revolution did not spread evenly or all at once. In addition, since
natural resources are distributed unevenly around the world,
technologies improved and economies grew at different rates.

In those countries where industrialization did take hold,
life for millions of people became safer and more secure.
Improved sanitation, reliable nourishment, safe housing, and
new medical treatments, especially vaccinations, all led to better health. Incomes rose, and people were able to enjoy a broad
range of goods and services. Many people lived longer, more
satisfying lives.

The outcome of these advancements was demographic
transition—the tendency of people to have fewer children as
their economic circumstances improve. Modern economists
and demographers recognize four stages of demographic transition, a phenomenon that occurs over several generations.

Stage 1: Large families are typical. Children are considered an asset because they can do work (on a
farm or in craft-based businesses) and care for their
aging parents. But death rates are high as a result of
childhood diseases and the hardships of rural life, so
fertility rates are also high to offset the death rate.

Stage 2: Advances in medicine and hygiene reduce
infant mortality and allow adults to live longer,

but the tradition of having many children remains intact. As a result, the population growth rate increases. In each generation there are still more people having more children, far exceeding the replacement rate, while at the same time the death rate is falling.

Stage 3: Population density forces people off farms and into cities. In cities, having many children is a disadvantage—housing is crowded and maintaining a large family is expensive. As people realize this and, at the same time, better their circumstances, the birthrate begins to drop.

Stage 4: Having reached a higher standard of living by taking advantage of more opportunities for education and employment, people choose to have smaller families. With health and income stable, children are no longer needed to earn money for the family or take care of the elderly. The birthrate falls to or near replacement level, resulting in low or zero population growth.

A Titanic Collision

While the Industrial Revolution carried populations through the demographic transition, raising the standard of living for many, it also brought some unpleasant consequences. Children worked long hours in dirty factories. Working-class people did not have access to the fruits of prosperity enjoyed by the middle and upper classes. The air and water in industrial cities were fouled by busy factories. As the architect William McDonough and the environmental scientist Michael Braungart have written, "Victorian London was notorious for having been 'the great and dirty city,' as Charles Dickens called it, and its unhealthy environment and suffering underclasses became hallmarks of the burgeoning industrial city. London air was so grimy from airborne pollutants, especially emissions from burning coal, people would change their cuffs and collars at the end of the day."

Though the Industrial Revolution saw great technological advancements, its side effects led to air pollution and overcrowding, as can be seen in this depiction of Victorian London.

And so, as the Industrial Revolution picked up steam, it brought signals of trouble and disaster along with progress and optimism. McDonough and Braungart describe the collision to come:

> In the spring of 1912, one of the largest moving objects ever created by human beings left Southampton, England, and began gliding toward New York. It appeared to be the epitome of the Industrial Age—a potent manifestation of technology, prosperity, luxury and progress. It weighed 66,000 tons. Its steel

hull stretched the length of four city blocks. Each of its steam engines was the size of a town house. And it was headed for a disastrous encounter with the natural world. . . . The vessel, of course, was the *Titanic*, a brute of a ship, seemingly impervious to the forces of the natural world. In the minds of the captain, the crew, and many of the passengers, nothing could sink it.

Many environmental scientists believe we are now in the midst of that "disastrous encounter with the natural world." They believe that Earth's growing population will only make that disastrous encounter worse. However, there are sturdy, inspiring reasons to believe that we can create a positive, more sustainable relationship with the natural world. New green technologies can shrink our ecological footprint. Our economies can consume less, while nations, working together, can restore the health of the air, water, and soil. There are also many reasons to believe that we can reach an optimal population on Earth and meet the needs of all the world's people. But to fulfill our hopes, to take intelligent steps into the future, we first need to understand how our technologies and our great numbers are straining our relationship with nature.

Three

Too Much, Not Enough

Nature works for us. We rarely think twice about breathing air or where our water comes from or having enough to eat; but all those things, and more, are provided by Earth's biodiversity, the web of living things that makes this a hospitable planet.

One way to appreciate this intricate web is to follow how water flows through it. "Water cycles constantly between atmosphere, land, and sea," writes biologist Yvonne Baskin. "It is breathed out pure and fresh from the evaporation of oceans, from the open waters and soils of the continents, and by the life processes of plants and animals, a great exhalation of water vapor powered by the energy of the sun. Aloft, this vapor cools and condenses into clouds, rains out, and makes its way back to the sea."

Through this process, known as the hydrological cycle, water supports and sustains every living thing. Our bodies run on fresh water. Forests and wetlands, the cradles of biodiversity, thrive with ample rainfall. They, in turn, provide clean air. Plants, animals, and microorganisms, all composed mostly of water, generate and preserve rich soils. Without each of

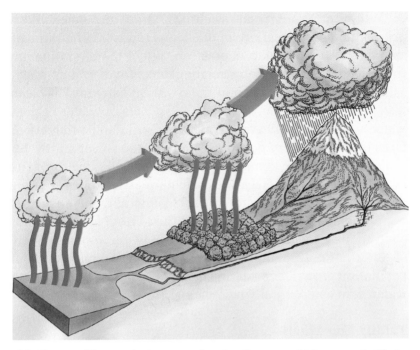

This diagram illustrates the natural cycle of water, which supports life in all ecosystems.

these natural processes, we cannot sustain our lives or feed the world. A water-rich, healthy biosphere is essential to our good health.

Ecologists, with some worry, are trying to understand how population growth and surging consumption affect this intricate web of life. They wonder, too, how we will fare if we take more than nature has to give.

Water Smart?
While giving life, water can also tell us a lot about how we live. The ways in which a city or a region uses and conserves water can help reveal, among other things, that locality's relationship with nature—its ecological footprint. Recall how the overconsumption of water in the American West has changed the natural flow of the Colorado River, damaging biodiversity downstream.

When environmental scientists study ecological footprints, they pose a variety of questions to arrive at an understanding of how human populations affect the environment.
In exploring a population's relationship to water, they might
ask: are there plentiful fish in the rivers and streams? Is clean
water abundant or scarce? Does the soil absorb water or does
water wash it away? Are farmlands fertile and productive?
Does everyone, every day, have enough food to eat and water
to drink? Does the economy help or harm the health of the
environment? Ultimately, these small questions lead to a big
one: is a population "water smart"? Generally, the answer is
no, not usually. In the ideal world, the natural cycle of water
continuously replenishes the water supply. But Earth's supply
of water has natural limits. In many places the combination of
population growth and soaring demand is claiming more fresh
water than can naturally be replenished.

Taking Too Much
In wealthy, industrialized nations, scarcity is usually due to
overconsumption and pollution, both of which diminish the
world's supply of fresh water. In the United States the daily
consumption of water for drinking, industry, agriculture,
sanitation, and a variety of other uses equals 100 gallons per
day for every man, woman, and child. Increasingly, there is
not enough to go around. Even once vast sources of water
are under stress. In the American West, the demands on the
Ogallala Aquifer, a deep underground basin beneath parts of
seven states, has lowered the reservoir's water level by as much
as 100 feet (30.5 meters). The basin may soon be pumped dry.

The United States is not the only heavy user of natural
resources. With a population of 1.3 billion, China exerts con-
stant pressure on its environment. Its consumption of timber,
minerals, oil, and water is unrivaled. The province of Sichuan
now possesses less than 10 percent of its original forests. Loss
of biodiversity is accelerating. Water is especially scarce; more
than 60 million people have limited access to clean water.

China is going to great lengths to address water scarcity.
In effect, it is "replumbing" the nation, building a network

A cotton farm in Texas draws its irrigation water from the dwindling Ogallala Aquifer.

of canals and tunnels that will reroute its water supply. The canals will extend thousands of miles, funneling water from the river deltas and floodplains of southern China to Beijing, where dry, wind-borne soil often shrouds the city in dust. Rivers will be rearranged and whole ecosystems undone. The project's long-term impact on the environment is unimaginable.

Overconsumption and scarcity are global problems. As world population has surged, nations large and small have used natural resources as if they were grains of sand on the beach, virtually free and in limitless supply. From Los Angeles to Tokyo, Brussels to Dhaka, we all take part in these extravaganzas of consumption.

Fast-growing economies have often fueled great progress, bettering the lives of millions. But as environmental scientists warn, it appears that there are just too many of us, using too much, too fast. While nature gives, the needs of billions leave a colossal footprint on the Earth.

As China builds its network of canals and tunnels to reroute its water supply, it also disrupts ecosystems, damaging the natural environment.

Raising the Stakes

Must economic growth cause environmental harm? Economists and scientists regularly debate this question. Some say economic development can provide opportunities to enhance environmental protection. Others argue that economic growth always causes harm. One expert on population growth, Dr. Paul Ehrlich, believes the latter is true. "The struggle merely to support today's population at today's standards of living," he writes, "is causing environmental destruction on a scale and at a pace unprecedented in human history." Population growth and overconsumption, he says, are "accelerating degradation and deforestation of land, depletion of groundwater, toxic pollution, biodiversity loss, and massive atmospheric disruption [all of which] are wrecking the planet's machinery for producing the basic material ingredients of human well-being."

Economists with a more sunny outlook say that economic growth can improve environmental protection. They argue that higher standards of living bring better education and environmental benefits, such as safe, healthful food, clean drinking water, and effective sanitation. Improved quality of life creates an increasing demand for green technologies and environmentally friendly development. These changes, in turn, can lead to better jobs and a rising standard of living. In other words: green follows green.

But then there's the industrial world's voracious appetite for oil. Jeffrey Sachs, who described the meteoric rise of the fossil fuel economy, mentions some of the results of this trend:

> By mobilizing a vast store of energy, fossil fuels . . . unlocked the mass production of goods and services on a scale beyond the wildest dreams of the preindustrial era. Modern energy fueled every aspect of the economic takeoff. Food production soared as fossil fuel energy was used to produce chemical fertilizers; industrial production skyrocketed as vast inputs of fossil fuel energy created equally vast powerhouses of steel, transport equipment, chemicals and pharmaceuticals, textile and apparels, and every other modern manufacturing sector.

But all the takeoffs and skyrocketing, all the benefits of the fossil fuel economy, are exacting an enormous cost: the global disruptions of climate change.

Cranky Climate

Climate change presents an extraordinary challenge. It changes the game. This is so because climate change so powerfully disrupts the water cycle. All those connections between water, plants, animals, and soil are changed when the planet overheats.

Population growth and overconsumption raise the stakes because climate change is caused by human activity: most importantly, the burning of fossil fuels. The burning of coal, oil, gasoline, and natural gas releases carbon dioxide into the air.

Carbon dioxide has always been part of the Earth's atmosphere, and that has been a good thing for us. Along with other "heat-trapping" gases, carbon dioxide absorbs the heat of the sun as it reflects off the surface of the planet. These gases are like the windows of a greenhouse. They let the sun's energy in and they release some, creating a stable level of warmth that supports life. A balance of carbon dioxide, water vapor, and other greenhouse gases has long maintained Earth's temperature.

During the past century, however, as world population and consumption have grown, the burning of fossil fuels and forests has steadily increased the amount of heat-trapping gases in the atmosphere. These added gases are enhancing the natural greenhouse effect, which captures more heat, warming the Earth. The result is not just a warmer Earth, but a new era of rapid and unpredictable change. Because climate change disrupts the water cycle, it affects weather patterns. Climate scientists studying the buildup of greenhouse gases have concluded that human-induced changes in weather patterns will bring a

A Canadian pulp mill, which burns fossil fuel, releases carbon dioxide into the air.

Due to climate change, a lake of meltwater develops on a glacier.

variety of hazards. They see warming trends causing dangerous disruptions in water and food supplies, the natural processes of ecosystems, and the health of coastal communities. Nearly all these changes result from overconsumption.

We have already begun to see the effects. In fact, volatile, cranky weather has become common. Other effects are potentially more severe. Environmental scholar Lester Brown has cataloged what he believes are some of the most disruptive changes. "Mountain glaciers are melting almost everywhere. Himalayan glaciers that feed rivers that irrigate the rice fields of China and the wheat fields of India are fast disappearing." Melting ice sheets will cause the sea level to rise 39 feet (12 m), which will put many of the world's coastal cities underwater. More than 600 million coastal dwellers will be forced to move—they will be "climate refugees." Meanwhile, record high temperatures, crop-withering heat waves, and drought are already disrupting agriculture. In 2002 worldwide grain harvests fell 90 million tons.

The worldwide effort to address climate change is contentious and complicated. As *New York Times* reporter Andrew Revkin writes, it is a "momentous tussle between rich and poor countries over who steps up first and who pays most for changed energy menus." Revkin, who calls this debate the global "climate divide," continues:

> Emissions of carbon dioxide per person range from less than 2 tons per year in India, where 400 million people lack access to electricity, to more than 20 in the United States. The richest countries are also best able to use their wealth and technology to insulate themselves from climate hazards, while the poorest, which have done the least to cause the problem, are the most exposed.

Having Too Little

The populations of developing nations are exposed to climate change in a variety of ways. Many impoverished countries are in regions where natural resources, such as fertile soil, are in short supply. People in these countries often lack access to the food, water, and sources of energy that would allow them to lift themselves out of poverty. Climate change will intensify their problems because the causes of food and water shortages—drought and high temperatures—will continue at higher levels.

And so the populations of developed and developing nations face the same challenges from opposite directions. Both are concerned with the ways in which population growth puts pressure on the natural world. Both want to be able to meet their needs and enhance their quality of life. But while the wealthy nations contend with the effects of overconsumption, the rapidly growing, developing nations struggle with the problems due to having too little. For example, today more than 1.1 billion people do not have regular access to clean water. By 2015 scientists project that 40 percent of the world's population, roughly 3 billion people, will live in impoverished countries where water is in short supply.

Ethiopians wait for water rations during a drought.

The director of the United Nations Food and Agriculture Organization, Dr. Jacques Diouf, has aptly explained the impact of water scarcity:

> Lack of access to adequate, safe water limits our ability to produce enough food to eat or earn enough income. It limits our ability to operate industries and provide energy. Without access to water for drinking and proper hygiene it is more difficult to reduce the spread and impact of life-threatening diseases like HIV/AIDS. Every day 3,800 children die from diseases associated with a lack of safe drinking water and proper sanitation.

51

Fog Catching

With water crises unfolding almost everywhere, creative, innovative ways to harvest and use water are more important than ever. One of the most simple, effective ways to collect water is called fog catching, a low-tech way to supply fresh water in areas with negligible rainfall.

According to *WorldChanging*, towns and villages in Chile, Nepal, and southern Africa are already benefiting from fog-catching arrays, a network of "fine nets that are stretched vertically between poles, with a gutter at the bottom." As fog drifts through the nets, it condenses and runs down the nets into the reservoirs. Depending on the amount of water collected, *WorldChanging* author Alex Steffen explains, the reservoirs can "supply homes, irrigation systems, or whole villages with water.

"The systems require little maintenance—they're inexpensive devices with no moving parts and no need for power. The water needs no treatment to be potable; in fact it is usually much cleaner than all but the best well or river water."

In a Chilean village, fog catchers collected up to 25,000 gallons of water per day throughout their first year of operation. They were so productive that the village stopped importing water by truck and began growing gardens and fruit trees.

In rural Kenya, water scarcity is a daily concern. In fact, the lack of water is so acute that women sometimes take their daughters out of school, assigning them, instead, to walk miles every day to get the families' supply of water. As a result, many girls never finish their education. This limits their choice of jobs in adulthood and keeps women in subservient roles, since they lack the knowledge or experience to participate in their communities on an equal basis with men who have completed their schooling. Uneducated girls also marry earlier and have more children than those with even a few years of education. This is one of the ways in which poverty and scarcity influence population growth.

Thankfully, there are ways out of this poverty trap. As African development expert Margaret Catley-Carlson has noted, if given a chance, young women will seize the opportunity to go to school and take positive steps to get out of the cycle of scarcity and poverty:

> In the foothills of the Abedares in Kenya, I met a former teacher in a village school who had quit because both she and her students had to venture farther each day to fetch water. We were together at the opening of a village water pipe where sweat equity had dug trenches and the Canadian International Development Agency had supplied pipes to bring water to the village from the mountains. Happily, she said she and her girls were going back to school.

A seemingly small change such as this can have a big impact. When young people and their families do not have to spend so much energy fulfilling their basic needs, they can begin to attend to other important requirements. While children return to school, parents freed from the backbreaking work of hauling water can spend time finding less grueling, more profitable ways of making a living. These changes can ripple through communities, releasing people from the poverty trap. When the scarcity of resources goes unaddressed, however, there are other, far less positive ripples.

Ripples of Scarcity

"If we are facing a future of water scarcity," writes environmental scholar Lester Brown, "we are also facing a future of food scarcity." When water is running low and food is scarce, soil takes a beating. Soil is not just dirt. It is alive with microorganisms and rich in minerals, both of which nourish the growth of plants. Good soil also captures and holds rainwater and secures deep roots. Plants in fertile soil make food from sunlight. Their leaves capture solar energy, and, with water, transform it into the sweet roots and leafy greens that feed humans and countless other creatures.

In the world's poor countries, however, good soil is as scarce as clean water. Many poor countries, especially those in the hot, dry environments along the equator, do not have very fertile soil to begin with. Equatorial lands are often punished by drought, and with climate change droughts are growing worse. Much of the land is only marginally fertile, but it must be farmed to provide large populations adequate food. As a result, soils are often overused.

Deforestation also causes soil loss. Without any protective vegetation, without forests to capture rainfall and release it slowly into irrigating streams, soil dries and blows away. As fertile land becomes increasingly scarce, as it is in the Amazon and sub-Saharan Africa, farmers cut deeper into the forest, planting crops in marginal land, which is often washed away by floods. Kenyans have been known to plant on hillsides so steep that farmers are sometimes injured when they fall off their narrow, terraced fields. As forests are cut down, crop yields plummet and food is scarce. In the meantime, vast acres of forest have been lost, and with them, their rich biodiversity.

The effects of such trends are worsened because the Earth's population is growing by 74 million people a year. As Lester Brown writes,

> [T]his is not a trivial addition to world population
> . . . when cropland is becoming so scarce and water
> shortages are now cropping up. Not only is almost
> all the projected population growth going to be in

These girls in Malawi work the dry soil on their family's farm.

the developing world, but the vast majority of the nearly 3 billion people to be added by 2050 will come in countries where water tables are already falling and wells are going dry. This is not a recipe for economic progress and political stability.

What is the recipe? Is there a recipe for a world in which 6 billion people, at all times, have access to enough nutritious food, enough clean water, and enough prosperity to maintain healthy and active lives?

Bridging the Divide

Many environment and development experts believe that "sustainable development" offers the recipe that will bridge the divide between rich and poor countries. The term is usually used to describe economic development that meets the needs of current generations without compromising the ability of

Can Biotechnology Feed the World?

Biotechnology is not new. For thousands of years farmers have practiced selective breeding, pairing the best animals to produce offspring that will enhance the herd. But most biotech scientists say that selective breeding is a sledgehammer compared with the sharp scalpels they use today.

The first big success of biotechnology came with the design of scientifically precise hybrid plants. In the 1970s, these hybrids led to the Green Revolution, an era of higher crop yields that ended hunger for millions.

By today's standards, even that looks like child's play. In 2010 biotech scientists created an Atlantic salmon genetically engineered to grow twice as fast as a regular salmon. Skeptics call the fish "Frankenfood." They say engineered genetic changes of any kind put the food supply and the natural world at risk. Genetically modified crops, for example, can mingle with native species and change them forever, with unknown effects. And, they add, twenty-first-century biotechnology is a radical departure from traditional breeding, which aims to select valuable traits from species that naturally mate. Genetic engineering, on the other hand, transfers the genes of one organism to another with which it does not naturally mate. Since those changes are irreversible, skeptics believe they are not changes worth making.

Those who support biotechnology say that precise genetic engineering is a proven way to reduce disease, protect plants from insects, and increase the food supply to ease world hunger. Genetic engineers are also working on vaccines and other pharmaceuticals. Besides, they say, we have all been eating genetically modified food for years, from rice to soybeans to taco shells.

There is a third perspective in the debate, the precautionary principle. It suggests that biotech foods may well be a boon to humanity. Pest-resistant crops, for example, may help farmers build a bridge between today's pesticide-ridden farmlands and tomorrow's resurgent, organic soils. But we don't know. And since there is no scientific certainty about the effects of bioengineering, is it possible to balance its benefits with the risk of causing irreversible harm?

future generations to meet their own needs. In other words, sustainable development gives equal weight to economic growth and environmental protection.

That's the simplest definition, and the one originally used when the United Nations introduced the idea in the 1980s. But sustainable development also carries a spirit of optimism. People engaged in sustainable development want to secure the needs of all future generations; to protect human well-being and the health of the natural world; to equally share the Earth's resources; and to pay special attention to giving all the world's people the freedom to choose the lives they want to live.

It is well known that overpopulation and overconsumption damage the environment. So, in a crowded world with an enormous appetite for natural resources, how do we achieve the goals of sustainable development? How do we protect the environment and meet human needs? The challenge can be addressed from two directions: First, by slowing population growth. Second, by reducing consumption.

Four
An Alliance with Nature

Our story began with a young man from rural Nigeria leaving a failing farm to move to Lagos. His journey is part of a great exodus of the world's poor from rural regions to fast-growing cities. It is the most momentous population change in human history. Just over one hundred years ago there were only a few urban areas of one million people; today there are twenty-seven megacities with populations exceeding 10 million. The migration continues day by day, and there is no end in sight. Yet, even with this great migration to cities, rural populations are also growing fast. These surges in population growth are most pronounced in developing countries, where poverty and human pressures on the environment are already intense.

Can these trends be reversed? Population experts and environmental scientists believe that they can. They recognize two complementary changes—economic development and a transition from large to small families—that could set a new course. These specialists are hopeful because they have seen these changes before, identifying them collectively as the "demographic transition," a process in which populations stabilize over time, moving from rapid to zero population growth.

The key factor is prosperity. Prosperity always eases population growth. "Uncrowding," in turn, always eases pressure on the environment and allows more people to meet their basic needs. Some countries have reached the goal of zero population growth, some are on their way. Yet many countries are trapped on the bottom rung of the economic ladder. Their populations continue to grow while their environments provide less and less sustenance. This dire scenario is not inevitable, however. Some poor countries, against great odds, are changing course.

Escaping the Poverty Trap

The climb up the ladder out of poverty begins when communities gain access to the basic social services, such as education and health care, that lead to small families. This is important because, first of all, small families put less stress on the home environment, such as a family farm. When there are fewer mouths to feed, farmers feel less pressure to wring all they can from their fields, which has the effect of protecting soil fertility. This, in turn, means that the land can provide for generations rather than just a few seasons, thus ending the need to cut down forests in attempts to replace overused land. With more to go around—more food, more water, more nourishment—the whole family enjoys better health and more productive lives.

When small families become the norm, entire countries can benefit. Many sustainable family farms, spread throughout a province or a region, add up to healthier ecosystems on a large scale. Meanwhile, healthy ecosystems provide the nature-based services (clean air, fresh water, healthful food) upon which a people and a country cannot only survive, but thrive.

These ecosystem services are the foundation of the second hopeful prospect for easing population growth: economic development. Economic development, which allows people to escape the poverty trap, is not just an accumulation of money. The term refers to the progress a country makes over time as it seeks to provide the goods and services that satisfy the needs of its population. That includes good roads, transportation, and reliable sanitation, as well as jobs, schools, health care, and a safety net for sick or impoverished citizens.

When these public goods are in place, they give people the stability to hold jobs and start businesses. With better health care, mortality rates drop significantly and the need to have many children for labor and to provide care for the elderly becomes far less urgent. As a result, more people are better off, families tend to be smaller, and a country's ecological footprint shrinks. However, when public goods are not in place, the speed of population growth is dangerously high and the scale of environmental destruction almost unlimited.

The New Dust Bowls

Following the journey of the Nigerian farmer from country to city is a good way to take the measure of this unruly phenomenon. When he walked away from his family's farm, the young man left behind his parents and six brothers and sisters. A family of nine is not the least bit unusual in rural Nigeria, nor in rural regions around the world.

Impoverished farm families tend to be large for several reasons. First of all, the mortality rate is high. With a strong likelihood that one or even a few children will get sick or die, having more children guards against a shortage of able-bodied helpers on the farm. The work requires many hands because it is labor intensive and time-consuming; farm families have to grow and raise nearly all they eat. Feeding more mouths seems like a reasonable trade-off when the loss of one family member could have a devastating effect on the productivity of the farm. In addition, no one but the family is available to care for aging parents, so again, a big family looks like a good bet.

But these bets offer diminishing returns. Often, farms are divided among many elder brothers, who then have even less land on which to scratch out a living for their own large families. Over time, as more children have more children, population growth skyrockets. Then the land is overused and soil loses its fertility, which causes a cascade of environmental problems that extend way beyond the borders of individual farms.

In sub-Saharan Africa, as farms have grown less productive, families have switched to raising livestock, with a view to supplying meat to developed countries and to meet their own desperate need for protein. To accommodate the grazing needs of cattle and sheep, land must be cleared, and the number of grazing animals soars with the needs of growing human populations. In Nigeria alone, the livestock population grew from 6 million in 1950 to 145 million in 2006. As the forage needs of all these cattle and sheep overwhelm the carrying capacity of the land, vast expanses of grassland are being converted to desert. In fact, soil erosion and desertification—in the Middle East and Asia as well as Africa—are occurring on a scale never before seen, or even imaginable.

Tracking dust storms is one way scientists can measure the steady advance of deserts. In 2005 NASA tracked an African dust storm that stretched roughly 3,300 miles (5,300 kilometers) and covered an area larger than the United States. Some storms deposit dust as far away as the Caribbean, where

As farms become less fertile, many in Africa have chosen to raise cattle instead. However, overgrazing has turned once-lush grasslands into desert.

they damage coral reefs. Scientists estimate that 2 billion to 3 billion tons of soil blow from Africa's dust bowls each year, draining the continent of its biological wealth. It is no better in Asia. China loses 3,600 square acres of land (1,460 sq ha) to desert each year.

An Alliance with Nature

It's no wonder that hundreds of millions of people are migrating to cities. But with urban populations rising, fast-growing cities present another web of ecological problems. As is true in Lagos, most of the world's booming cities were intended for hundreds of thousands of people, not tens of millions. Migrants, with no place to go, become urban pioneers, building patched-together homes and establishing neighborhoods on wetlands, floodplains, forest land, and unstable hillsides. Floods, mudslides, and ecological crises soon follow. In his global survey of the spread of urban poverty, *Planet of Slums,* author Mike Davis reports that in Latin America, 90 percent of the sewage from overcrowded cities is dumped untreated into rivers and streams.

Some of these *favelas*, or slums, extend outside the city into greenbelts and farmland. In India, more than 123,000 acres (50,000 ha) of valuable cropland is lost to urbanization each year. Ecological reserves and protected watersheds are also imperiled. New settlements in Mumbai extended far enough outside the city to have colonized a national park. Deep in the park, on the far urban edge, people are sometimes attacked by leopards. On one occasion a leopard attacked a city bus. These seemingly isolated problems add up to a big one: the destruction, in cities, of what Davis refers to as an "alliance with nature." A city that has an alliance with nature is devoted to protecting the environment, its natural support system. Protecting wetlands, for example, offers many benefits.

Wetlands are part of the ecosystems of many coastal cities. They filter pollutants from wastewater and runoff, preserving clean shorelines and fisheries. They absorb heavy rainfall, preventing flooding and its dire impact on homes, businesses, and human lives. Wetlands also provide breeding and feeding areas

A hillside *favela* in Rio de Janeiro, Brazil, is home to thousands of "urban pioneers," poor migrants who build makeshift communities on public land.

for countless creatures—from migrating songbirds to turtles to waterfowl—supporting an intricate web of biodiversity. Even urban economies derive benefits from healthy estuaries, which are home to valuable seafood, such as oysters and crabs.

Greenbelts and open space on urban edges protect valuable agricultural land. Mike Davis notes that "Asian cities, as seen from the air, have been traditionally surrounded by a bright green corona of high productivity market gardening." These green urban edges are intact ecosystems where nature does its work, where the water cycle is untrammeled and the flow of nutrients from soil to plants to soil supports healthy farms and forests.

When cities protect nearby forests, they also preserve another valuable resource: clean water. Nearly all of New York City's drinking water comes from a forested watershed in the mountains north of the city. If the city had not helped protect the unspoiled forest, it would be spending millions of dollars each year to treat its drinking water chemically. The fact that

The city of New York protects its watershed as a means of providing clean drinking water for its residents.

clean water is abundant in New York, a city of 8 million, shows the power of an alliance with nature. It is also a beacon of hope for megacities struggling with the impact of overcrowding.

Restoring Nature, Building Prosperity

An alliance with nature is also the foundation of economic development. Healthy ecosystems provide good jobs and good health, both of which encourage small families and ease population growth. As population growth eases, human pressure on the environment eases as well. That's what environmental scientists call a virtuous cycle: it supports life at every turn. As virtuous cycles take hold in communities, they can end the vicious cycle of overpopulation, poverty, and environmental harm.

Restoring the environment creates nature-based jobs and community wealth. In the Philippines, a community is replant-ing mangrove forests. Healthy mangrove forests anchor rich coastal ecosystems. Their far-reaching tangles of roots spread out above the surface of the water, providing nesting places for seabirds and shelter for fish. The mangrove forests also stabi-lize shorelines, protect against erosion, and build islands.

As the Philippine mangrove forests recover, fish and shell-fish have been reintroduced into the shallow sea, improving biodiversity. Birds have returned to nest. The crab popula-tion has dramatically increased. Local fishermen now manage aquaculture farms where selected crabs mature and are then sold at markets. Many other fish are returning to the mangrove forests as well. Slowly, a fertile ecosystem is being restored. Since the restoration of the mangrove forest began, the income of fishing households has doubled. Ecotourism also offers new sources of income in these Philippine coastal communities.

Agroforestry has also taken hold. Agroforestry is a way to reforest and rebuild soil at the same time. The process begins by planting trees on the borders of farmlands. As trees grow into forests, they can begin to do what forests do best: build soil depth, capture water, protect biodiversity, and dramatically reduce soil erosion. Agroforesters also plant trees and crops in the same fields. At first the trees grow slowly, allowing wheat

Biologists from around the world inspect newly reforested mangroves in the Philippines, which restore the environment, shelter birds and fish, and provide nature-based jobs..

or corn or millet to grow in the sun while tree roots hold the soil. After the crop has been harvested, the saplings flourish and later drop leaves onto the field. The leaves rot, providing mulch and nitrogen, both of which build and nourish the soil.

Both of these methods of agroforestry support economic renewal. They improve the productivity of farmlands, providing surplus produce to sell at village and urban markets. In a community in Cameroon, agroforestry increased wheat yields by 200 percent and potato harvests by 300 percent. New forests also provide tree seedlings, another source of income. In turn, the sale of produce and seedlings supports ongoing reforestry in Cameroon, where farm families now plant up to 120 trees a year. As community wealth grows, so do benefits like

good schools, clean water, and good health. And as these positive changes spread, a modest, but vital prosperity takes hold. By protecting the environment, poor countries are taking the first step out of the poverty trap.

A Bright Green Future

Green technology is another tool for nature-based development. In Bangladesh, a country of 145 million people, community investments in renewable energy are reducing air pollution and greenhouse gases while also creating new jobs. The green energy program provides homes with a simple, affordable solar power system. The home system consists of a photovoltaic panel that converts sunlight to electricity, a battery that stores the electricity, and connecting devices that route electricity to specially designed lights. This is a powerful new tool and a remarkable leap forward in a country where 70 percent of the population has no access to electricity and most people light their homes with heavily polluting kerosene oil.

Community biogas plants, which convert animal waste to clean fuel for cooking stoves, are also part of the energy program. In Bangladesh, wood is the primary cooking fuel. As the country's population has exploded, the increased need for wood has led to the curse of the developing world, deforestation. Now clean fuel is radically changing communities' impact on the environment, improving the life and prospects of hundreds of thousands of people. And there is an added bonus: each biogas customer is asked to plant five trees in the family's backyard.

The energy program has also created economic opportunity. The program is financed with small loans, known as microcredit, from Grameen Bank, a microfinance bank. The interest on the loans is very low, allowing even poor households to purchase the solar systems. In addition, the bank supports each community's ability to sustain a clean energy economy on its own. It finances technical training for young people, who install and maintain solar systems. Other training programs invite young women to learn how to build and repair the components of photovoltaic panels and solar batteries. Each of these jobs provides steady income and stimulates the local economy.

Meanwhile, the availability of light and electricity gives artisans more time to produce goods and offers entrepreneurs the means to create new businesses. There are phone-charging shops, TV halls, and computer training centers. Over time, a boost from the microfinance bank has generated myriad opportunities, all built on environmental protection. What began in 1997 as a modest program to provide electricity to 225 homes now powers 135,000 homes and brings electricity to 5,000 new homes every month. By 2015 local entrepreneurs are expected to have fully adopted the green energy business plan, marketing, installing, and maintaining solar systems for a million homes. And then there are the backyard trees, some 3 million and counting.

A Little More for Everyone
The Bangladeshi clean energy initiative is unique in its inclusion of women. Inviting women to participate in new enterprises is rare in the developing world, where women are rarely encouraged to work outside the home. Research shows, however, that population growth slows when women have access to education and employment.

Creating stable or optimal populations is ultimately about individual lives and the betterment of life for all people. In times of population change, the individual lives most affected, and most influential, are the lives of women and girls. The status of females—their well-being and the way they are regarded in the world—determines how much freedom women have in decisions about bearing children. In many poor countries women have little freedom and often have large families.

Most women, however, whether poor or wealthy, "aren't seeking *more* children, but more *for* their children." In other words, when given the chance, women will choose smaller families so their children will not only survive, but thrive. Along with improving children's health, bearing fewer children also improves the health and well-being of women. This is especially true in poor countries, where mothers often get sick or die from the physical trials of having many children.

Goals for Humanity

In the modern world, it would be almost impossible for any developing nation to pull itself out of poverty on its own. The key lies in a combination of change within the nation and help from others. In 2000 world leaders met to establish concrete goals to combat poverty and improve economic growth in low-income countries so that the world's most vulnerable people would have a chance at a better quality of life. The participants adopted eight Millennium Development Goals, each with specific targets intended to be met by 2015.

- Eradicate extreme poverty and hunger by increasing the availability of good jobs (including work for women and young people) and improving nutrition, especially for young children.

- Achieve universal primary education by equalizing the ratio of boys and girls in school so that all young people are able to read and write.

- Promote gender equality and empower women by equalizing ratios of boys and girls in schools and by improving opportunities for women in the workplace and government.

- Reduce child mortality by increasing rates of measles immunization, and enhance health care to children under the age of five.

- Improve maternal health by offering better access to health care during pregnancy and childbirth and by providing education and resources for family planning.

- Combat tuberculosis, malaria, and other infectious diseases by increasing programs for education, prevention, and treatment.

- Ensure environmental sustainability by restoring biological resources, reducing pollution, improving access to clean water and sanitation, and improving quality of life in city slums.

- Set up a Global Partnership for Development, establishing internationally accepted systems of trade and governance to reduce debt and bring technology to developing nations.

A 2010 United Nations report summarized the program's mixed results for its first decade:

Important progress has been made and there are many notable successes that offer encouragement. In all but two regions, primary school enrollment is at least 90 percent; about 80 percent of children in developing countries now receive a measles vaccine and 1.6 billion people have gained access to safe drinking water since 1990.

But there is still a way to go. More than one billion people are living on less than a dollar a day, and nearly a quarter of all children in developing countries are undernourished. In one hundred countries, boys and girls do not have equal opportunities to go to school.

The choice to have fewer children is beneficial for the whole family. It allows for more for everyone: sufficient food and water, better health, more opportunity. Multiplied by the choices of many women, the benefits ripple, helping ease poverty, improve the well-being of communities, and relieve pressure on the environment.

Three Wishes

Education is the first important step toward more well-being for everyone. In many developing countries, girls normally don't have access to education, but given a chance they will seize an opportunity to go to school. Consider the experience of Tererai Trent of Zimbabwe, a young woman profiled by *New York Times* journalists Nicholas Kristof and Sheryl Wu Dunn.

When Tererai was a young girl, she did household chores and herded cattle, while her brother, Tinashe, went to school. Tererai pleaded to go to school, but her father would not allow her to attend. So Tererai studied her brother's schoolbooks and taught herself to read and write. She did his homework every night.

Tinashe's teacher soon figured out that he was not doing his own homework. Learning that Tererai was doing the work, the teacher told the children's father that his daughter was a prodigy and talked him into allowing her to go to school. But less than year later, Tererai was sent off to be married.

Tererai's husband did not allow her to return to school, and so she practiced her reading by looking at scraps of old newspaper. Encouraged by an aid worker, Tererai began to secretly study on her own. She wrote her goals on a piece of paper, placed the paper in an old can, and hid it under a rock. Her dreams? She wanted to earn a college degree, a master's degree, and a Ph.D.

Tererai took correspondence courses, started working for an aid agency, and slowly saved money. She was a brilliant student and was encouraged to apply to several colleges in the United States. She was accepted at Oklahoma State and earned the first two of the degrees she coveted. She is now working on her doctorate at Western Michigan University. Each time

Tererai achieved one of her goals, she went home, dug up her can, and put a check beside that item on her list.

Having finished her coursework for the doctoral degree, Tererai is completing a dissertation about the prevention of infectious diseases among the poor. She will become a productive economic asset in her country and a significant figure in the battle for better health care in Africa. And when she returns home, she will dig up her can and put a check beside the final goal on her list, her impossible dream fulfilled.

Tererai is one of many women in the developing world who have found a way to go to school. This has a profound ripple effect. As Tererai said, "If I educate myself, then I can educate my children."

Schools Rock

Educated girls can change their communities. Recall Margaret Catley-Carlson, who learned that the Kenyan teacher and her students had gone back to school when the girls no longer had to spend their days fetching water. She was so pleased to see them return because she knew that getting an education would dramatically improve their lives. She noted that uneducated girls marry earlier and have more children than those with even a few years of education. On the other hand, "a primary education for girls has resulted in more community improvement than any other factor." In communities where girls have been able to go to school, local farms produce more food, family nutrition is better, the environment is well protected, incomes are higher, and family health is improved. These are the first steps out of poverty, and they change the lives of the whole community—women, men, and children.

Going to school offers other social benefits as well. In developing countries, free lunch programs draw children to school, where they receive basic nutrition their parents cannot provide. It is well known that hungry children are sick more often and do not learn as well. They may also suffer lifelong cognitive and physical problems. The good news is that a simple school lunch can solve these problems and give children a better chance to achieve their dreams.

Because of economic hardships, thousands of girls in Africa do not attend school, a misfortune that negatively affects entire communities.

A Billion Trees

Education can also lead directly to environmental protection. The Kenyan Nobel Peace Prize laureate Wangari Maathai, who is also a committed environmentalist, was one of the first women in Africa to earn a Ph.D. and the very first to hold a department chair—one of the highest achievements for a scholar—at Kenya's largest university. Drawing on her education and prestige, she started the Greenbelt Movement, which is devoted to forest restoration in Africa.

Kenya, where a growing and impoverished population was cutting down vast swaths of forest for fuel and fresh farmland, was a country well suited to host the first programs in the

A Population Campaign: Promoting Prosperity in Kenya

The governments of populous countries have long encouraged small families. China's and India's population campaigns are the most well known, but African nations, too, have sought to ease population pressures. According to a report aired on *NOVA*, Kenya was the first country in sub-Saharan Africa to view population growth as serious barrier to economic prosperity, and in the late 1960s the government began developing the first national family planning campaign in the region. Kenya's official population policy calls for matching population size with available resources, but decisions on family size are left up to individual families.

While the Kenyan government formulates official strategies on family planning, promotion of the message and means of family planning falls mainly to local health care offices. By all accounts, the country's approach has been successful. The average number of children per woman has dropped to around four from around eight in the 1980s. That is one of the fastest-ever national declines in family size.

Advertisements for Kenya's population campaigns, which target both men and women, tend to frame the need for family planning around the evident realities of population growth such as overuse of land and scarcity of jobs. The campaigns are particularly active in rural areas. Where populations are growing most rapidly, the rewards of education are great.

Children in Kenya hold saplings that they will plant as part of the
Greenbelt Movement.

Greenbelt Movement. As in Nigeria and China, the advance of
deserts was not far behind the deforestation activities of many
desperately poor people. Maathai decided to tackle the problem
head-on. She won a small grant and hired women from all over
Kenya to plant thousands of trees, a boundary of green to stop
the steady loss of land to the great African dust bowls.

Soon Maathai was hiring hundreds of women, and then
thousands. Over the last thirty years, the Greenbelt Movement
has planted 30 million trees and given livelihoods to tens of
thousands of women. Countries all over the world have followed
in her footsteps. Inspired by the Kenyan environmentalist's

international "Billion Tree Campaign," Mexico has pledged to plant 250 million trees. Ethiopia is planting 60 million. Senegal, another 20 million. In all, nearly half a billion trees have been planted.

The New Entrepreneurs

The Greenbelt foresters are not alone. Women in poor countries all over the world are finding innovative ways to create jobs and go to work. Many, like the Bangladeshi solar entrepreneurs, are creating successful enterprises with microcredit loans. "Phone ladies" in rural villages are getting loans to buy a single cell phone, which becomes the pay phone that serves the community. Some use the phone to stay in touch with relatives, others to grow their own businesses. Fishermen, for example, use the phone to call various markets to see who is paying the best price. It's a small business, but over time the phone ladies pay off their loans, make a modest profit, save, and spend money in the village. Everybody wins.

With employment, women's status soars. Working outside the home allows a woman to contribute money to her household. Suddenly, her contribution to her family's prosperity becomes more visible. Her independence and her earning power win respect and give her a voice in family affairs, including family size. Planning together, parents can choose how many children to have, and when to have them. They can raise the children they determine to have with the best possible future in mind.

Consider a story, related by the economist Jeffrey Sachs, about a group of businesswomen in Bangledesh. With a microloan, they started a successful enterprise making and selling food and clothing near the city of Dhaka. There were thirty-six women in the group. Sachs and a colleague later visited the women to learn how the business enterprise had changed their lives. They found that most of the women had decided to have only one or two children and some had none.

That is a dramatic change in Bangladesh. Most of the women in the group had grown up with six or seven brothers and sisters. Now they were choosing very small families.

"This social norm was new," Sachs observes, "a demonstration of a change of outlook and possibility so dramatic that [we] dwelt on it throughout the rest of our visit."

The new norm impressed Sachs because it showed that overcrowding and its negative environmental impact are not inevitable. There was great promise, he noted, in new jobs for women, in women's spirit of independence, in rising literacy among girls. With better access to health care and family planning, women and their partners had choices about family size that had not been available to the couples' parents. "With fewer children," Sachs notes, "a poor household can invest more in the health and education of each child, thereby equipping the next generation with the health, nutrition, and education that can lift Bangladesh's living standards in future years." Here was a country that had begun to turn itself around, taking the first steps out of poverty toward a brighter future.

Five
Remaking the Way
We Make Things

All the problems we face can be dealt with using
existing technologies. And almost everything we
need to do to move the world economy back onto
an environmentally sustainable path has already
been done in one or more countries.
—LESTER R. BROWN, Earth Policy Institute

As developing countries escape poverty and ease population
growth, they face a problem: when nations become more prosperous they are likely to consume more, which can reverse
the environmental benefits of uncrowding. The United States
and the European Union, where wealth has stoked the fires of
consumption, are good examples. In fact, the consumption
of natural capital by wealthy, populous nations worldwide is
so vast that it is difficult to comprehend.

We are familiar with the huge appetite for energy of the
United States and China; but these problems are just the tip of

the iceberg. Paul Hawken, a coauthor of *Natural Capitalism: Creating the Next Industrial Revolution*, describes America's extravagant consumption of natural resources. "Industry moves, mines, extracts, shovels, burns, wastes, pumps, and disposes of 4 million pounds of material in order to provide one average middle-class American family's needs for a year. In 1990 the average American's economic and personal activities mobilized a flow of roughly 123 pounds of material per day—equivalent to a quarter of a billion semitrailer loads per year." This includes fuel, construction materials, farm and forest products, and industrial minerals and metals. Those are the materials consumed. The amount of waste is equally impressive. He continues by saying,

> Americans waste or cause to be wasted nearly 1 million pounds of materials per person per year. This figure includes: 3.5 billion pounds of landfilled carpet, 3.3 trillion pounds of carbon in CO_2 gas emitted into the atmosphere, 19 billion pounds of polystyrene peanuts, 28 billion pounds of food discarded at home, 360 billion pounds of organic and inorganic chemicals used for manufacturing and processing, 710 billion pounds of hazardous waste generated by chemical production, and 3.7 trillion pounds of construction debris.

The European Union nations, meanwhile, consume an astronomical amount of materials: it would take three Earths to provide the same standard of living to the rest of the world. The moving, mining, extracting, shoveling, burning, wasting, pumping, and disposing of natural resources is very much like that of the United States.

Changing Course
As with poverty and population growth, overconsumption and the environmental harm it causes are not inevitable. While easing population growth addresses "too many," environmentally sustainable economies address "too much." By doing more with less, by using resources carefully and

efficiently, sustainable economies offer both prosperity and environmental protection.

What is an environmentally sustainable economy? First of all, like the nature-based enterprises in the developing world, it is an economy that works with nature to provide public goods. It does not destroy the environment while meeting the needs of its population. It values and restores the natural world while providing transportation, schools, jobs, health care, and economic opportunity. It uses natural capital thoughtfully and seeks to ease humanity's impact on the Earth.

The Industrial Revolution provided many of these goods and services, but the result was a set of conditions that worked against nature. The architect William McDonough often says that the motto of the Industrial Revolution, and our economies today, is: "If brute force doesn't work, you're not using enough of it." Why not use environmental smarts rather than brute force? Why not renew our alliance with nature? Or, to put it another way, how do we build a better *Titanic*?

Recall the mighty *Titanic*, a 66,000-ton behemoth with steam engines the size of a townhouse. Its steel hull stretched the length of four city blocks. It was a brute of a ship, seemingly impervious to the forces of the natural world. People thought nothing could sink it. Well, we know how that turned out. So let's design a new ship, one that will not have a disastrous encounter with the natural world.

We'll start with those steam engines. They certainly represented the state of the art, big and impressively powerful. But they burned acres of coal and belched carbon dioxide— lots of carbon dioxide. Given our warming world, the iceberg that sank *Titanic* is probably gone, but climate change presents even more danger. Our ship is heading into a perfect storm. The world is consuming more fossil fuels every year and will continue to do so as population grows. We need new forms of energy.

Riding the Wind

The first problem is a supply problem: the world is running out of fossil fuel. By most accounts we have already passed "Peak

One recent casualty from drilling for offshore oil was the 2010
Deepwater Horizon disaster.

Oil": the moment in which the world production of oil dropped
below world demand. Therefore our supply is limited. That is
why the search for oil has grown increasingly difficult and
dangerous. The Perdido Platform in the Gulf of Mexico operates
in 8,000 feet (2,440 m) of water and drills thousands more
feet into the seabed. Some deepwater platforms drill in 10,000
feet (3,050) m of water and another 25,000 feet (7,620 m)
into the seafloor. The *Deepwater Horizon* disaster, which
killed eleven men and spilled an estimated 4.9 million barrels
of oil, shows just how dangerous and costly oil exploration
can be. New forms of clean, renewable energy present no such
challenges. They work with nature, not against her, easing
the environmental impact of even large populations.

Numerous technologies are capable of generating renewable energy. Wind turbines generate power with the rotation
of their blades. Solar cells capture the energy of the sun and
transform it into electricity. Along coastlines, ocean cur-
rents drive power-generating turbines. Solar thermal plants

concentrate sunlight with an array of lightweight mirrors, which activate engines that produce electricity. Cars, too, can be powered by the sun. By the process of electrolysis, solar thermal plants create hydrogen out of water. Hydrogen-powered cars are extremely energy efficient—and their only "exhaust" is water. Plug-in hybrid cars, already on the market, can travel 40 miles (65 km) on electricity alone—electricity generated by the wind and the sun.

These technologies are not science fiction. Denmark produces 20 percent of its power with wind turbines. Sixty million Europeans now get their residential electricity from wind farms. Iceland heats nearly 90 percent of its homes with geothermal energy. Wind farms in Texas generate electricity

In Spain, renewable energy is generated with wind turbines and solar panels.

Wasteland to Parkland

Conserving natural resources is an excellent way to preserve the health of the Earth for future generations. But what about the trail of waste we inherited—all the things used and thrown away that have piled up in mountainous heaps at the landfill? One solution is to turn those wastelands into parklands. That probably sounds a little unappetizing. Who would want to play Frisbee or have a picnic at the dump? A team of landscape architects working at New York City's Fresh Kills landfill would answer: Why not everyone? These innovators are in the process transforming the vast garbage dump, one of the largest in the world, into a wildlife sanctuary and public park three times the size of Central Park. It is a formidable challenge.

Fresh Kills, on Staten Island, received New York City's waste for fifty-three years—26 million pounds of commercial and household waste every day. It was piled so that high Fresh Kills was the highest point on the eastern seaboard.

The team of architects, from the firm Field Operations, will cap the four mountainous heaps with a protective polymer liner, which will then be covered with several feet of topsoil and seeded with native plants. Plants will also be used to help clean nearby wetlands. Meadows and woodlands will be cleaned and tended to aid in the recovery of the land. Over the years the park's edge will become a densely planted ecological corridor. There will also be sport fields, trails for walking and cycling, and equestrian paths. Kayakers will be able to paddle the restored waterways. Visitors will be able to watch migratory birds or have lunch at a park restaurant.

The park makers' goal is simple: to create a pleasing place for people while restoring the natural world for generations to come. That's a legacy entirely different from any that could have been imagined even a few years ago. It is a leap of imagination that creatively meets the challenges of our fast-growing world.

equal to that of twenty coal-fired power plants. In California, new solar energy projects will generate enough electricity to power nearly 600,000 homes. With the greatly increased use of technologies such as these, reversing climate change, our biggest consumption problem, is within our grasp.

Remaking the Way We Make Things

Using renewable energy is sustainable and smart. It shows what we can accomplish by learning how nature works. It's a good model for redesigning our world and restoring the health and wealth of the natural world. That is the goal of environmentally sustainable economies: to use nature as a model to completely remake the way we make things.

With our enormous appetite for natural resources, redesigning materials and rethinking how we use them can be building blocks of sustainability. Recycling, for example, has been taken to a whole new level. While recycling paper products is a great idea, designers are now making valuable consumer products that can be used again and again. High-tech carpets are designed to be recovered by their manufacturer when they show wear, then remade into new, equally valuable carpets. With this process the 3.5 billion pounds of discarded carpet now going to waste would be replaced by an equivalent weight of fully recyclable materials that will never see a landfill.

There are other building blocks of sustainability. The second largest furniture maker in the United States remanufactures every kind of furniture it has ever made into brand-new, high-quality products. In the fast-growing tech industry, many companies are designing every part of the next generation of computers to be reused or recycled. European car manufacturers disassemble entire cars and trucks and use their parts to make new automobiles. All these renewable products and materials are remaking the throwaway economy. They change the wasteful, one-way trip to the landfill into a smart, renewable flow of goods and services. They are another way to curb consumption and reduce stress on the environment.

Big and Green

Architecture is another sphere in which nature-based design is reversing overconsumption. Architecture literally creates the building blocks of our world. Architecture is not just the Taj Mahal or the Empire State Building. Architecture is everywhere. Your home, your school, your library—all are architecture. Stores and soccer stadiums, hospitals and city halls—all are architecture. And because it is everywhere, and because growing populations need more and more buildings, architecture consumes even more energy and material than any other human activity. In fact, architecture accounts for 70 percent of U.S. energy consumption and 40 percent of CO_2 emissions. Worldwide, building construction consumes 40 percent of all materials used, 20 percent more than manufacturing.

But the impact of architecture can be transformed by environmental design. Year by year, green buildings are becoming more the norm than the exception. Instead of overconsuming energy, green buildings can now be zero-carbon structures, adding virtually no greenhouse gases to the atmosphere. Many use recyclable materials, as well as recyclable carpets and furniture. In fact, the next generation of buildings draws on new ideas from every field. There are buildings powered by the sun and the wind. Some are heated with geothermal energy, which rises up from the earth. Others are cooled with water from nearby rivers. Some have sensors, ensuring that rooms are lit only when they are occupied. Others are illuminated mostly by natural light. There are "green walls" of plants and trees, which filter indoor air.

Green roofs are sprouting everywhere, on factory rooftops as well as the tops of high-rise buildings. A green roof is a layer of soil and an array of plants that insulates buildings, keeping them cool in the summer and warm in the winter. Green roofs also create microhabitats for birds and bees, and pleasant, refreshing places for people to rest and relax. The green roofs on many buildings are equipped to absorb rainfall and funnel it to giant cisterns underground. The water in the large holding tanks is then used for sanitation or the irrigation of indoor gardens, which also cool and clean the air. This is

The Brooklyn Grange commercial farm is located on the rooftop of a building in Long Island City, New York. It produces fifteen different crops, including lettuce and kale.

a truly beneficial alliance. It employs ideas rather than brute force. While dramatically reducing consumption, a green roof creates a place that is good for people *and* nature, offering a means of providing sustainable homes and buildings for a fast-growing world.

The lessons learned from tapping renewable energy, making new materials, and designing green buildings are being applied in every walk of life. Innovators from dozens of fields, often called green designers, are working to turn our world around. They want to show how consuming less and reducing our giant footprint is beneficial for all. They see ways to build a bright green future and renew the places damaged by the mistakes of the past. They want to clean the air and rebuild the soil; conserve water and energy; grow enough food to feed the world; restore industrial wastelands; protect biodiversity, and more.

Cities of the Future

As millions of people surge to cities, the need for sustainable cities grows. In China the need is especially pressing. China has more than ninety cities of a million or more people. Many have inadequate water and energy, gray skies, and choked, dirty rivers. On an island near Shanghai, the Chinese government is trying to create a new kind of city. There, architects, engineers, and city planners have been developing a cutting-edge, ecologically friendly metropolis.

The city, Dongtan, is designed to house a million people. It will have no cars. Its rapid transit system will produce zero

Visitors walk on the promenade of Millennium Park in Chicago, which is built on a 24-acre green roof.

greenhouse gas emissions, and its buildings will be "zero carbon." It will harvest rainwater and recycle its water as well. The city's wastes will be used to generate energy—no landfills necessary. China plans to build four of these green cities and hopes they will be models for a bright urban future.

While China plans a new city, many cities are already going green. They don't have just one big, green building, they have many. Zero carbon is the new standard for all buildings, as well as for transportation, manufacturing, city lighting, and other services. Industrial wastelands are being turned into parks. In some cities there are acres of green roofs. The celebrated Millennium Park in Chicago is actually a 24-acre (9.7 ha) green roof. Vancouver, British Columbia, has a Sustainability Precinct. Once an industrial area, it is now a thriving neighborhood of green buildings, parks, and gardens. It has a busy shopping street, as well as bike paths and footpaths. There is a clean, efficient light-rail system, so there are few cars, no carbon emissions, and lots of fresh air. These are just a few of the new tools and ideas for creating sustainable cities.

More Crop per Drop

Agriculture uses 70 percent of the global water supply. Less than a quarter of that 70 percent is absorbed by plants.The draining of the Ogallala Aquifer is just one example of the world's unquenchable thirst. Making better use of water, doing more with less, would help address overconsumption in the developed world. It would also ease food and water shortages in countries with fast-growing populations. How do we get more crop per drop?

Surface irrigation, which funnels water in open canals, has been the method of choice for millennia. Mesopotamia invented this form of irrigation and collapsed when it failed. It is a wasteful method because it allows nearly half the water funneled to canals to evaporate. *Drip irrigation* is an effective alternative, watering far more crops with far less water. Drip irrigation, which runs underground, carries just the right amount of water, just where it is needed. In Jordan, drip irrigation increased cucumber and tomato yields by 20 percent. In India, it produces abundant crops of bananas, cotton, sugarcane, and sweet potatoes.

Israel saves water in several ways. Farmers there use drip irrigation as well as recycled water and greenhouses. Greenhouse agriculture recaptures water transpired from plants and evaporated from the soil. Water circulates much as it does in nature.

The Ground under Our Feet

Imagine a city that creates new farmland. In Liuzhou, China, that's just what architects hope to do. Urbanization is putting a great deal of pressure on China's best farmland, which is quickly being lost to development because it is close to cities. Croplands are especially close to Liuzhou, which used to be an agricultural center. So architects have designed new buildings that will house the growing population *and* create farmlands on the rooftops. These new urban fields are designed to provide acres of fresh, fertile soil, and to support crops of soybeans and sugarcane as well as rice paddies. In a country that could lose as much as 25 percent of its farmland by 2020, rooftop farms could feed millions.

Will the world be able to feed billions? Robert Engelman of Worldwatch Institute believes we might:

> For most of the 6 million or so years that human-like creatures have stood on two feet, we walked in nature and fed ourselves from its bounty without overwhelming effort. By increments, learning all the way, we came to where we are today—with numbers and cleverness that give us the power to unwittingly submerge coastlines under rising seas and to untwist the thread of life itself.

But if the world of the future will be warmer, and perhaps biologically poorer, he writes, "we can nonetheless begin the long process that will allow nature and its life-sustaining resources

More Water for More People

Water shortages in poor, populous countries mean that millions of people do not have enough water to drink, let alone for agriculture. In many places there is not even plumbing. The "soft path"—no plumbing necessary—offers an alternative. By following the soft path, *WorldChanging* notes, people can meet their water needs with simple technologies. The Q-Drum, for example, simplifies the task of fetching water. A cylindrical container with a hole in the middle, like a stack of doughnuts, the Q-Drum can be easily rolled instead of carried. It relieves the backbreaking work of carrying water, and since it holds 50 liters (13 gallons), it saves hours of time. A child could fetch water for the family *and* go to school.

When water is too far away, new human-powered pumps can efficiently draw clean groundwater to the surface. Muscle-powered pumps can even be fun. The Roundabout PlayPump is powered by a merry-go-round. No joke. When kids play on the merry-go-round, the rotation drives a pump that pulls water from a well up into a water tower. Faucets on the water tower allow easy access to clean water.

Water that is not clean can be purified by solar Watercones. The Watercone uses the sun's energy to evaporate water, which condenses on the inside of the cone and drips through a porous filter. When the cone is flipped, you can pour clean water into a container. The Watercone can remove all waterborne pathogens as well as harmful chemicals. It can also desalinate seawater, removing salt to make the water suitable for drinking. These simple, soft-path technologies are saving untold numbers of people from everyday thirst.

to reverse their retreat. Population . . . has always been a critical part of life. It will always be. . . . [But] with a bit of luck and an understanding of our place in nature, humanity's moment on this rich but finite planet may stretch out for longer than we can now imagine. . . . Wanting not more people, but more for all people, we might find ourselves at home again, with more nature than we thought possible, in an Eden we can keep."

Notes

Chapter One

p. 8, ". . . most of the world's population . . .": Mario Polese, "Urbanization and Development," *Development Express*, no. 4, 1997.

p. 8, ". . . 2.9 billion urban dwellers . . .": United Nations Population Fund (UNFPA), State of the World Population 2007 (New York: 2007), p. 1.

p. 9, ". . . our numbers will likely surpass 7 billion.": U.S. Census Bureau, "World Vital Events," n/d, www.census.gov/ipc/www/popnote.html (Accessed May 19, 2010).

p. 11, ". . . making megacities work . . .": Alex Steffen, *WorldChanging: A User's Guide for the 21st Century* (New York: Abrams, 2006), p. 283.

p. 14, ". . . human activity is putting such a strain . . .": WorldWatch, "The Unsustainability of Current Consumption Patterns," *State of the World 2010* (New York: WorldWatch, 2010), p. 3.

p. 16, "Population growth constantly pushes the consequences . . .": Engelman, "Population and Sustainability.

p. 17, " . . . a young woman nearly dies . . .": *NOVA*, "World in the Balance," www.pbs.org/wgbh/nova/worldbalance/about. html (Accessed October 5, 2010).

p. 20, ". . . in this unequal world . . .": Engelman, "Population and Sustainability."

p. 21, "I really like what the car brings . . .": quoted in Maureen Fan, "Creating a Car Culture in China," *Washington Post*, January 21, 2008, www.washingtonpost.com/wp-dyn/conten/article/2008/01/20/AR2008012002388html (Accessed September 21, 2010).

p. 23, "There is no escape . . .": quoted in Steffen, *WorldChanging*, p. 19.

Chapter Two
p. 30, "Dust clouds boiled up . . .": Timothy Egan, *The Worst Hard Time* (New York: Houghton Mifflin, 2006), p. 5.

p. 36, "The steam engine marked the decisive turning point . . .": Jeffrey D. Sachs, *The End of Poverty: Economic Possibilities for Our Time* (New York: Penguin Press, 2005), p. 33.

p. 39, "Victorian London was notorious . . .": William McDonough and Michael Braungart, *Cradle to Cradle: Remaking the Way We Make Things* (New York: North Point Press, 2002), pp. 20–21.

p. 40, "In the spring of 1912 . . .": McDonough and Braungart, *Cradle to Cradle*, p. 17.

Chapter Three
p. 42, "Water cycles constantly . . .": Yvonne Baskin, *The Work of Nature: How the Diversity of Life Sustains Us* (Washington, DC: Island Press, 1998), p. 73.

p. 46, "The struggle merely to support today's population . . .":
Paul Ehrlich et al., *The Stork and the Plow: The Equity Answer to
the Human Dilemma* (New York: G. P. Putnam's Sons, 1995),
p. 1.

p. 47, "By mobilizing a vast store of energy . . .": Sachs, *The
End of Poverty*, p. 33.

p. 49, "Mountain glaciers are melting . . .": Lester Brown, *Plan
B 3.0: Mobilizing to Save Civilization* (New York: W. W. Norton,
2008), pp. 48-49.

p. 50, ". . . a momentous tussle between rich and poor . . .":
Andrew Revkin, "Global Warming," *New York Times*, http://
topics.nytimes.com/top/news/science/topics/globalwarming/
index.html?scp = 2&sq = climate % 20divide7st = cse (Accessed
October 23, 2010).

p. 50, "Emissions of carbon dioxide per person . . .": Revkin,
"Global Warming."

p. 51, "Lack of access to adequate, safe water . . .": Jacques
Diouf, quoted in Food and Agriculture Organization, "Coping
with Water Scarcity," March 22, 2007, http://www.fao.org/
newsroom/en/focus/2007/000521/index.html (Accessed May
20, 2010).

p. 52, ". . . Chile, Nepal and Southern Africa . . .": "Steffen,
WorldChanging, pp. 192–193.

p. 53, "In the foothills of the Abedares . . .": Margaret Cately-
Carlson, "Working for Water," in McDonald and Jehl, eds.,
Whose Water Is It Anyway?, pp. 68–69.

p. 54, "If we are facing a future of water scarcity . . .": Brown,
Plan B 3.0, p. 79.

p. 54, "This is not a trivial addition to world population . . .":
Lester Brown, *NOVA* interview, "World in the Balance:

Voices of Concern," www.pbs.org/wgbh/nova/world
balance/voic-brow.html. (Accessed October 5, 2010).

Chapter Four

p. 63, ". . . 90 percent of the sewage from overcrowded cities. . . ":
Mike Davis, *Planet of Slums* (New York: Verso, 2006), p. 121.

p. 63, ". . . alliance with nature . . .": Davis, *Planet of Slums*,
p. 134.

p. 65, "Asian cities, as seen from the air . . .": Davis, *Planet of
Slums*, p. 135.

p. 69, ". . . aren't seeking more children . . .": Robert Engelman,
More: Population, Nature and What Women Want (Washington,
DC: Island Press, 2008), p. 8.

p. 70, ". . . adopted eight Millennium Development Goals . . .":
United Nations Development Program, "What are the
Millennium Development Goals?" n/d, www.undp.org/mdg/
basics.stml (Accessed March 17, 2010).

p. 71, "Important progress has been made . . .": United Nations
Development Program, *Beyond the Midpoint: Achieving the
Millennium Development Goals* (New York: United Nations
Development Programme, January 2010), p. 3.

p. 73, "If I educate myself . . . ": quoted in Nicholas Kristof
and Sheryl WuDunn, "A Woman's Crusade," *New York Times
Magazine*, August 17, 2009, www.nytimes.com/2009/08/23/
magazine/23women-t.html (Accessed September 21, 2010).

p. 73, ". . . a primary education for girls . . . ": Cately-Carlson,
Working for Water, in *Whose Water Is It Anyway?*, p. 69.

p. 75, ". . . Kenya was the first country . . .": *NOVA*, "World
in the Balance: Voices of Concern." www.pbs.org/wgbh/nova/
worldbalance/campaigns.html (Accessed October 5, 2010).

Notes

p. 78, "This social norm . . .": Sachs, *The End of Poverty*, pp. 13–14.

p. 78, "With fewer children, a poor household . . .": Sachs, *The End of Poverty*, p. 14.

Chapter Five

p. 80, "Industry moves, mines, extracts . . .": Paul Hawken, Amory Lovins, and L. Hunter Lovins, *Natural Capitalism: Creating the Next Industrial Revolution* (New York: Little, Brown, 1999), pp. 51–52.

p. 80, "Americans waste or cause to be wasted . . . ": Hawken, Lovins, and Lovins, *Natural Capitalism*, pp. 51–52.

p. 81, "If brute force doesn't work . . .": quoted in McDonough and Braungart, *Cradle to Cradle*, p. 30.

p. 91, "For most of 6 million or so years . . . ": Engelman, *More*, pp. 241–242.

p. 91, ". . . we can nonetheless begin . . .": Engelman, *More*, p. 242.

p. 92, "The Q-Drum . . ." Steffen, *WorldChanging*, p. 192.

Further Information

Books

Dalton, Dave. *Environmental Migrants*. Chicago: Heinemann Library, 2006.

Desoine, Dana. *Humans and the Natural Environment: The Future of Our Planet*. New York: Chelsea House Publishers, 2008.

Obadina, Tunde. *Population and Progress* (Africa: Progress and Problems). Philadelphia: Mason Crest Publishers, 2007.

Stefoff, Rebecca. *Modern Humans*. New York: Marshall Cavendish Benchmark, 2007.

Stewart, Gail B. *Population*. Yankton, SD: Erickson Press, 2008.

Websites
High School Environmental Resources
www.epa.gov/highschool/
Worried about the impact of human population on the environment? The U.S. Environmental Protection Agency offers educational information and suggestions for making a difference in your community.

The Human Footprint
www.wcs.org/human footprint/
Compare ecological footprints in different regions of the world, and find out how your actions at home can have wide-reaching benefits.

Lights at Night
www.koshland-science-museum.org/exhib_lightsatnight/
Find out how satellite images of the Earth at night can reveal population change and it impact on the planet.

National Geographic's Eye in the Sky—Overpopulation
www.nationalgeographic.com/eye/overpopulation/over population.html
Learn more about the environmental impacts of human population from *National Geographic*'s detailed text, graphics, and video.

Young People and Climate Change
www.unfpa.org/webdav/site/global/shared/swp/english youthswop.pdf
Learn more about climate change in this publication, a supplement to the UN's State of World Population 2009, which was written for young people.

Earth's
Growing
Population

Bibliography

Baskin, Yvonne. *The Work of Nature: How the Diversity of Life Sustains Us*. Washington, DC: Island Press, 1998.

Brown, Lester R. *Plan B 3.0*. New York: W. W. Norton, 2008.

Davis, Mike. *Planet of Slums*. New York: Verso, 2006.

Diamond, Jared. *Guns, Germs and Steel: The Fates of Human Societies*. New York: W. W. Norton, 1999.

Economy, Elizabeth. *The River Runs Black: The Environmental Challenge to China's Future*. Ithaca, NY: Cornell University Press, 2004.

Ehrlich, Paul, and Anne Ehrlich. *One with Nineveh: Politics, Consumption and the Human Future*. Washington, DC: Island Press, 2004.

Ehrlich, Paul, *The Stork and the Plow: The Equity Answer to the Human Dilemma*. New York: G. P. Putnam's Sons, 1995.

Egan, Timothy. *The Worst Hard Time*. New York: Houghton Mifflin, 2006.

Engelman, Robert. *More: Population, Nature, and What Women Want*. Washington, DC: Island Press, 2008.

Fara, Patricia. *Science: A Four Thousand Year History*. Oxford: Oxford University Press, 2009.

Fernandez-Armesto, Felipe. *Civilizations: Culture, Ambition, and the Transformation of Nature*. New York: Touchstone, 2002.

Hawken, Paul, Amory Lovins, and L. Hunter Lovins. *Natural Capitalism: Creating the Next Industrial Revolution*. Boston: Little, Brown, 1999.

Jager, Jill. *Our Planet: How Much More Can Earth Take?* London: Haus Publishing, 2008.

Journal of International Affairs. *Water: A Global Challenge*. New York: Columbia University School of International and Public Affairs, Spring/Summer 2008.

Latif, Mojib. *Climate Change: The Point of No Return*. London: Haus Publishing, 2009.

Lovelock, James. *The Revenge of Gaia: Earth's Climate Crisis and the Fate of Humanity*. New York: Basic Books, 2006.

Maathai, Wangari, *The Green Belt Movement*. New York: Lantern Books, 2006.

McDonald, Bernadette, and Douglas Jehl, eds. *Whose Water Is It? The Unquenchable Thirst of a Water-Hungry World*. Washington, DC: National Geographic, 2003.

McDonough, William, and Michael Braungart. *Cradle to Cradle: Remaking the Way We Make Things*. New York: North Point Press, 2002.

Meyer, Bernd. *Costing the Earth? Perspectives on Sustainable Development*. London: Haus Publishing, 2009.

Munz, Rainer, and Albert Reiterer. *Overcrowded World? Global Population and Migration*. London: Haus Publishing, 2007.

Prahalad, C. K. *The Fortune at the Bottom of the Pyramid: Eradicating Poverty Through Profits*. Upper Saddle River, NJ: Wharton School Publishing, 2005.

Sachs, Jeffrey D. *The End of Poverty: Economic Possibilities for Our Time*. New York: Penguin Press, 2005.

Sen, Amartya. *Development as Freedom*. New York: Random House, 1999.

Shepard, Paul. *The Others: How Animals Make Us Human*. Washington, DC: Island Press 1996.

Smil, Vaclav. *The Earth's Biosphere: Evolution, Dynamics, and Change*. Cambridge, MA: The MIT Press, 2002.

Steffen, Alex. *WorldChanging: A User's Guide for the 21st Century*. New York: Abrams, 2006.

United Nations Centre for Human Settlements. *Cities in a Globalizing World*. New York: United Nations Centre for Human Settlements, 2001.

WorldWatch, *State of the World 2010*. New York: WorldWatch, 2010.

Index

Page numbers in **boldface** are illustrations.

Colorado River and, **13**
dust bowls, 30–**31**, **51**, 62–63
migration and, 31
Dunn, Sheryl Wu, 72
dust bowls, 30–**31**, **51**, 62–63

ecological footprints
carrying capacity and, 14
China, 21, 23
reducing, 41, 61, 88
water and, 43–44
economy
agroforestry, 67
Bangladesh, 68, 69
China, 21, 22–23
demographic transition and, 38–39
development, 23, 60–61, 66
ecosystems and, 66–68
education and, **74**
environmental destruction and,
45, 46–47
environmental sustainability and,
81, 86
fossil fuels and, 36
green technology and, 41
India, 17
Industrial Revolution and, 38
Kenya, 75
microcredit, 68, 69, 77
population surges and, 37
sustainable development, 55, 58
United States, 33–**34**
ecosystems
agriculture and, 60
carrying capacity, 14
climate change and, 49
ecological footprints, 14, 21, 23
economy and, 66–68
hydrological cycle, 42–**43**
Johannesburg Memo, 23–24
"Living Planet" report, **15**

United Nations Ecosystem
Assessment, 14
urban ecosystems, 65, 87–**88**, **89**,
91
water consumption and, 44–45,
46
wetlands, 63, **65**
education
agriculture and, 73
demographic transition and, 39
diseases and, 71
family planning and, 71, 78
India, 17, 20
Industrial Revolution, **36**
Kenya, 53, 73, **74**, 75
malnourishment and, 73
Millennium Development Goals
and, 70–71
women and, 69, 70, 72–73, **74**
Zimbabwe, 72–73
Egan, Timothy, 30
Ehrlich, Paul, 46
Engelman, Robert, 16, 20, 91, 94
England, 35, 39, **40**
erosion, 62–63, 66
Ethiopia, **51**, 77
European Union, 79, 80
exponential growth, 33, **37**

families
agriculture and, **17**, **55**, 60, 61, **62**,
67, 72
birth rates, 38, 39
education and, 39, 61
employment and, 77–78
Industrial Revolution, **36**
sizes of, **17**, 39, 59, 60, 61, 72
United States, 80
family planning, 16, 17, 20, 39, 69,
71, 72, 75, 77, 78
favelas (slums), 63, **64**

107

About the Author

Chris Reiter writes about sustainable development, architecture and design, natural history, and environmental issues for magazines, academic journals, businesses, and a variety of nongovernmental organizations such as the China-US Center for Sustainable Development, GreenBlue Institute, and the Biodiversity Project. He is the founding editor of an online environmental news service and has written articles and essays for numerous books, websites, and national publications, including *Natural History*, *Metropolis.com*, and National Geographic Society's *LandscopeAmerica*. This is his sixth book for young readers.